God Beyond Gender

God Beyond Gender

Crafting Inclusive Liturgy

Mary Kells

CANTERBURY
PRESS

© Mary Kells 2025

Published in 2025 by Canterbury Press
Editorial office
3rd Floor, Invicta House,
110 Golden Lane,
London EC1Y 0TG, UK
www.canterburypress.co.uk

Canterbury Press is an imprint of Hymns Ancient & Modern Ltd
(a registered charity)

Hymns Ancient & Modern® is a registered trademark of
Hymns Ancient & Modern Ltd
13A Hellesdon Park Road, Norwich,
Norfolk NR6 5DR, UK

All rights reserved. No part of this publication may be reproduced,
stored in a retrieval system, or transmitted,
in any form or by any means, electronic, mechanical,
photocopying or otherwise, without the prior permission of
the publisher, SCM Press.

Mary Kells has asserted her right under the Copyright, Designs and
Patents Act 1988 to be identified as the Author of this Work

British Library Cataloguing in Publication data

A catalogue record for this book is available
from the British Library

ISBN: 978-1-78622-631-0

EU GPSR Authorised Representative
LOGOS EUROPE, 9 rue Nicolas Poussin, 17000, LA ROCHELLE, France
E-mail: Contact@logoseurope.eu

No part of this book may be used or reproduced in any manner for the purpose
of training artificial intelligence technologies or systems.

Typeset by Regent Typesetting

Contents

Acknowledgements   vii

Part 1 What is Inclusive Liturgy, Why Do We Need it and How Do We Craft it?

1 Introduction: Context and Purpose   2
2 Defining Terms   7
3 Why? Why this Project and Why Me?   19
4 Principles and Practicals   23

Part 2 Putting it into Practice: Examples of Inclusive Liturgy

5 Examples and Resources: Getting Creative   38
  Confessions and Absolutions   39
  Collects   42
  Intercessions and Other Prayers   45
  Alternative Lord's Prayers   49
  Prefaces to Eucharistic Prayer   51
  Blessings and Endings   55

6	Examples and Resources: Services	57
	A Structure for Morning Prayer	57
	Service of the Word	59
	Service of the Word: Peterborough Diocese 2023	60
	Service of the Word in Lent: Wilderness	62
	Service of the Word: Scottish Episcopal Church	65
	Service of Lament and Hope: Synod Fringe Meeting	70
	Service of the Word: The Annunciation	73
	Service of the Word for Advent	76
	Service of the Word with Holy Communion	79
	A Liturgy of Becoming	86
	Service of the Word: Hope	92
	WATCH Conference	95
	A Liturgy of Transition	97
7	Conclusion	103
8	References and Resources	104

Appendix: Church of England Canon Law   113

Acknowledgements

I would like to thank WATCH (Women and the Church), whose idea it was to produce a guide to gender-inclusive liturgy, and whose encouragement and patience helped me keep going when, having volunteered to take on the task, I started to engage with the reality of delivering it alongside a busy day job. Their encouragement led me to have my work properly recognized and, instead of simply posting it on their website, seek a publisher. In particular, I would like to thank, from WATCH's Executive Committee, past and present: Professor Helen King, Canon Dr Felicity Cooke, the Revd Rosalind Rutherford, the Revd Canon Jennifer Thomas, the Revd Yvonne Clarke, the Revd Naomi Nixon and Ms Claire Creese, for reading drafts, having conversations with me and providing encouragement.

I am also grateful to the students of King's College, Cambridge, where I was Chaplain at the time of writing, for being themselves, and also for their lively engagement with my probing questions around inclusivity and gender identity. Conversations with Ash, Aoife, Sam, Robin and Gabriel were particularly helpful. Lastly, special thanks go to my conversation partner Taéodór (Teddy) Graham, whom I began to refer to as my trans consultant, I found their knowledge and opinions so valuable.

I am also grateful to the women Fellows of King's for their enthusiasm and encouragement, to Professor Jude Browne for a very helpful conversation about patriarchy, as well as to those Fellows who engaged in conversation with me over dinner. I am grateful to the Dean, the Revd Dr Stephen Cherry, for encouraging me along the publishing route and giving helpful advice. I am also grateful to Mrs Genet Elsom for cleaning my home for one particularly busy term, when I especially needed time to write.

And from my heart, I thank Aidan, my Generation Z offspring, for reading the first draft of my section on gender and sex and ensuring Mum wasn't embarrassing (if I am, it is of course my own responsibility), and my husband Alastair, whose capacity to supply *le mot juste* at crucial moments, together with his encouragement and wonderful capacity to cook meal after meal and give me the gift of time, were invaluable.

PART I

What is Inclusive Liturgy, Why Do We Need it and How Do We Craft it?

I

Introduction: Context and Purpose

> [U]s talk and talk bout God, but I'm still adrift. Trying to chase that old white man out of my head ... He been there so long, he don't want to budge.
> (Alice Walker, *The Color Purple*, pp. 177–8)

What image of God do you carry around with you? One formed by Christian Scripture and tradition, you may answer. Yet, it is increasingly recognized that Scripture and tradition are received within and through culture and language. This includes how we express our faith in our liturgy.

One aspect of our culture that we have been slow to problematize is patriarchy. This is partly because of its self-concealing nature.[1] Some confidently assert that talking about patriarchy is 'passé' (Manne, 2019, p. xx), but it is worth questioning to what extent the voices that assert this are those benefiting from patriarchal power. When alternative voices dare to declare that patriarchy is alive and well, and continuing to exert power over women's lives, who seeks to silence them, and why?

Although much has changed in recent decades, with increasing recognition of the need to tackle gender inequality, full equity has not been achieved and signs of everyday sexism remain prevalent. For example, in a recent WATCH (Women and the Church) event, a participant reported that the single man in the breakout group dominated the entire conversation, with no awareness he was silencing a group of women at an event that was designed to empower them. This has also been my recent experience.

---

1 This is highlighted by Kate Manne in relation to misogyny, a phenomenon she understands as serving to enforce the expectations and ideology of patriarchy.

And what about language? It is commonplace to address groups as 'you guys' even when women are present, and even when the group is entirely female. Seeking a more inclusive term for 'masterclass', I was told by a young man recently that he and his peers didn't see language like this as exclusive. 'Perhaps it's a generational thing,' he mused, when I said I did. Perhaps it is a gender thing. Susie Dent suggests that the inbuilt patriarchy in language is 'largely because of the voices that have been recorded over the centuries', and suggests it is women who have 'consistently been at the forefront of language change and yet not recognized for it', that 'women are about a generation ahead of men when it comes to language change'. Her comments accompanied Ellie Rees' discussion of her campaign to change the ubiquitous 'Dear Sirs' in business correspondence: 'We need a paradigm shift,' she suggested, 'yet it is slow to come' (*Women's Hour*, Radio 4, 9 November 2024).

Equity has not been achieved: this is visible in both language and action and is more than a question of discomfort. 'Medical misogyny' has been identified in a Parliamentary report (Women and Equalities Committee, 2024–25[2]), leading to a callous disregard for women's reproductive health. This would be no surprise to Caroline Criado-Perez (2019), who identified a wide range of areas in which women are disadvantaged by the ways in which our world is set up for men.

Levels of violence against women are so high that it has been declared a 'national emergency', as reported by BBC News on 23 July 2024 – the day the first national analysis of the scale of the violence against women and girls by the National Police Chief's Council was released. Why is this? Partly, they suggest, because young men are being 'radicalized' online by influencers such as Andrew Tate. Boys are being led by social media algorithms to these influencers and to violent content. The 2023 BBC Three documentary *Andrew Tate: the Man who Groomed the World?*

---

2 '"Medical misogyny" is leaving women in unnecessary pain and undiagnosed for years', 2024, at https://committees.parliament.uk/committee/328/women-and-equalities-committee/news/204316/medical-misogyny-is-leaving-women-in-unnecessary-pain-and-undiagnosed-for-years/ (accessed 04.04.2025).

has drawn attention to the way in which Tate and others like him groom men in domination techniques so that they can impose their will on women and control them, isolating them from their own agency and their own networks. A 2024 survey conducted by Plan International (UK) accessed the views of nearly 3,000 girls and young women (aged 12–21) in drawing attention to the effect of misogyny in the 'manosphere'. The survey reveals how a regressive and well-organized anti-rights and anti-gender movement curtails gender equality and human rights, blocks access to financial assets and condones gender-based violence. Of the girls and young women interviewed, 43% reported that they felt held back in life by limiting gender expectations. Some noted that saying girls can 'do anything' becomes meaningless when 'society is failing them by not enabling them to build the lives they want'. Only 5% reported that they feel 'completely safe' in public places.[3]

Our faith is inevitably influenced by the culture in which it is received and traditioned and – like our history, and even our present – it is resiliently patriarchal. We claim in our doctrine to worship a God beyond gender, yet the reality is that in our language and liturgy we conjure a man. Or as Elisabeth Johnson puts it, 'officially ... God is spirit and so beyond identification with either male or female sex, yet the daily language of preaching, worship, catechesis and instruction conveys a different message: God is male' (2002, pp. 4–5). For some, this renders the word 'God' irretrievably linked with patriarchy and thus irretrievably gendered as male. That is not the view I take in this book. Instead, I seek to enable us to recover our deep theological conviction that God is indeed beyond gender by representing this in our language.

Change is happening in our churches, but it is slow and piecemeal, and progressing at different rates in different denominations. The Methodist Church has composed an excellent guide to inclusive language.[4] In 2023 the Church of England's Faith and Order

---

3 At https://plan-uk.org/state-of-girls-rights-report.pdf, pp. 2–3, 5 (accessed 04.04.2025).
4 At https://www.methodist.org.uk/for-churches/the-inclusive-methodist-church/resources-events-and-support/resources/the-methodist-inclusive-language-guide/ (accessed 04.04.2025).

Commission proposed the development of new, gender-neutral liturgy, recognizing that praying to God the Father is not helpful for all and can be experienced as excluding and alienating for some. WATCH has been calling for this for some time. However, when the Archbishop of York Stephen Cottrell spoke publicly on this, it proved controversial and provoked a media storm. It is noticeable that, at the time of writing, the Commission has yet to report any findings. Elsewhere in the Anglican Communion, Bishops of the Episcopal Church in the United States recently voted against the Prayer Book Committee's recommendation that it adopt inclusive and non-ableist language (Paveley, 2024, p. 15). In the Roman Catholic Church, the Pope has addressed the question of desmasculinization of the Church and this may well open the door to new thinking about language. Lay Catholics are already pursuing this avenue.

This book speaks into this context, exploring how and why we might seek to make our language for God more gender inclusive, and it offers resources and examples for use and inspiration.

Although my own Church context is Anglican, my contention, *pace* the current Archbishop of York, is that we need to go beyond his recommendation of gender-neutral terms. While gender-neutral language is useful, powerful and biblical – offering understandings of God as rock, fire, cloud, presence (*Shekinah*) among others – I suggest this is not an adequate solution on its own, for three reasons.

The first reason is that we seek to worship a personal God. Gender is an integral part of our humanity and our relating, so a personal relating must take some account of this.

Second, we can take inspiration from Jesus, who used images drawn from our life experience to understand, approach and follow this God, and who revolutionized the understanding of God by introducing a human, familial term, Abba. Instead of being locked into his term, I suggest that we seek to emulate the courage to refresh the tradition that Jesus embodied.

The third reason is that of liberation, a key biblical theme and imperative. We are all made in the image of God, yet our language renders women, and all those who do not self-define as male, invisible. In order to correct an injustice and heal the hurts caused by this exclusion from the realm of the sacred, we need to bring fully into view those who have sat outside, or taken their value reflected through men rather than directly from God.

In this book, I offer liturgies that include female images and metaphors for God. These are already available to us in Scripture and tradition. I also take inspiration from the gender fluidity that the trans community offers us as a gift to understanding ourselves as human beings and explore where that might take us in approaching a God who is not fixed in any binary or any gender, but who relates to us through all our human experience. In addition, I use gender neutral language. In other words, I am aiming for both gender-less and gender-full, as this seems to me suitably complex and paradoxical to represent the God who is both transcendent and seeks to be understood.

Who is this for? The prayers and services offered here follow an Anglican pattern and are thus readily available to those who 'need material that is clearly shaped so that it will fit a recognizable place in a regular liturgy' (Morley, 1992, p. 7), but they can also be adapted to suit local context, either of denomination, or of a particular congregation, or, simply used as inspiration for those who wish to write more freely. This book may thus be a resource for anyone in a Christian church wishing to write or use liturgy that moves beyond exclusively male language.

These liturgies are found in Chapters 5 and 6. I begin in Chapter 2 by defining my terms, specifically 'gender and sex', 'patriarchy', 'liturgy' and 'inclusive'. I then explore more of the 'why' behind this project in Chapter 3. Chapter 4 presents practical tips and outlines some principles that can inform and assist us. These may be adapted to make worship more broadly inclusive of ethnicity, class or disability, for example. Following the concluding Chapter 7, Chapter 8 contains references and resources that have been useful to me. The Appendix gives details of Church of England Canon Law. This is designed primarily for Anglicans, but also reveals the context in which I myself operate, and how my writing fits within this.

2

Defining Terms

Gender and sex

What do we mean when we speak about 'gender'? I suggest we can only understand this by considering it in tandem with 'sex'. The subject is complex, and I will draw on a mixture of personal experience, conversation and writing on the subject, including Scripture, to arrive at my conclusions.

Gender has, for much of our history, been seen as the socially pliable meaning-creation that elaborates the physical reality of sex. Simone de Beauvoir's comment in *The Second Sex*, 'One is not born, but rather becomes, a woman' (1973, p. 301), was arguably the beginning of thinking about this distinction between sex and what has become known as gender.

When I was growing up, sex was indeed seen as physically incontrovertible, and gender an elaboration – a translation, to use Judith Butler's trope (2021) – into culture. I suggest that gender reflects not only social mores, but also power relations, reprising the ideology of the dominant group/s. Thus, as Caroline Criado-Perez suggests, 'much of what we think we know about gender is tied up with value judgements to which we never consented' (2015, p. 6).

I will now consider in more detail both the content of our understanding of gender and the way in which it connects to our sex.

Gender

As a young woman, I discovered both social anthropology and feminism. Recognizing the contingency of gender through these lenses was liberating. I learned to problematize how gender expectations attached to a whole lifetime. At birth, girls were dressed in pink and boys in blue, a colour coding that was expected to continue when they were old enough to choose for themselves. Girls and boys were expected to play in different ways and with different toys. In adulthood, women were expected to be 'good' mothers, submissive, gentle, nurturing, and remain in the domestic sphere, and men to be tough, sexual, capable, masterful, and successful in the public arena. Social rewards accrued to those who observed these category distinctions, and those who breached them attracted opprobrium. Gender expectations covered dress, sexual behaviour, leisure and work (both paid and unpaid), and also the emotional care-taking work required in relationships (detailed by Kate Manne, 2019). I thus observed a clear binary distinction in place covering the whole of how we live our lives.

However, understandings of gender have varied historically. As Helen King so forcefully reminds us, bodies exist only in history. Thus: 'inescapably, we can only think about our bodies and make sense of them in terms of the beliefs and theories of the period in which we live' (2024, p. 1). One historical difference is in the primacy of sex over gender. While today we understand sex as primary, Thomas Laqueur (1992, p. 8) suggests that up until the eighteenth century, *gender* was seen as the primary 'reality', to which bodily differences merely pointed (see also Økland, p. 169).

I now have a 21-year-old son, and I work in a university context with Generation Z students. I am finding that these stereotypes have begun to be broken apart in the space of a generation. Gender is a tool of social control, but can also be a means of rebellion. The most striking development is, arguably, the rejection of the gender binary itself. Today, in the West, gender is increasingly likely to be seen as a continuum, with male/female accompanied by categories such as non-binary, transgender, genderqueer, and so on. Facebook offers over 50 gender options in its drop-down menu. Gender is increasingly seen as a construction, a performance, a choice, characterized by intersectional variability.

This isn't as new, however, as we might think. First, in the global context, indigenous North Americans recognize a non-binary group of people known as 'two spirited'. In Polynesia, 'fa'afafines' are assigned male at birth but have both masculine and feminine gender traits. In Thailand and South Asia, a third gender is also recognized. In Thailand, 'Kathoey' are males who choose to live as female; and in South Asia, 'Hijira' men dress in traditionally feminine clothes but view themselves as neither male nor female. We might also consider the biblical category of 'eunuch', discussed in Matthew 19.12, which offers us an alternative category of maleness, one in which sexual potency has been removed but maleness remains.

We live in gender-complex times, historically, geographically and, perhaps especially, in the current moment. Increasingly, within our Western 'social imaginary',[1] individuals are encouraged to travel on a journey to claim their own, authentic gender identity. With the decline of traditional religious practice, this has perhaps become a spiritual journey of the modern age, one towards a different kind of 'truth'.

This 'truth' is, of course, disputed. Gender in the West is contested territory. Some hold to an 'essentialist' position, whereby male and female are seen as stable, fixed categories, sharing something inherent and universal, regardless of place, age and culture. The rise of 'complementarianism' in the Anglican Church, arguably a response to this current trend towards a new kind of gender self-identification, is an example of an essentialist position. It regards women and men as having different natures and therefore of necessity inhabiting different roles. We can also see this in the Vatican's characterization of current thinking about gender as a gradual process of denaturalization (2019).

By contrast, the journey of self-discovery that these responses are reacting to can be located within 'constructivism', which views gender as a performance, a construction, with so much contextual and intersectional variation that there is no meaningful common ground.

It is worth noting that not all essentialist positions are conservative, as radical feminists such as Mary Daly have seen female as a universal category, the content of which she and others have

---

[1] Charles Taylor's term referring to 'the way ordinary people "imagine" their social surroundings', expressed in images and stories rather than theory (2007, pp. 171–2).

explored very differently. The distinction between essentialist and constructivist positions is not the only source of debate.

My own position is to recognize both the power of the shared, universal category of woman/female, and the extent to which we play with, manipulate, construct what this means in our own context and for our own lives. Serene Jones terms this 'strategic essentialism' (2000, pp. 42–7). I also highlight the power factors inherent in any self-identification that limit this self-construction. We operate in a context, a point Simone de Beauvoir (1973) acknowledged.

Sex

For most of us living today, sex has been seen as binary, unequivocal, so visible that it can be assigned at birth. Biology, as Dupré notes, has been 'a fertile breeding ground for essentialism' (2021, p. 58). This supports the idea that sex is how our bodies *are* and gender is how we explore this culturally. However, Laqueur illustrates excellently the limitations of this in relation to anatomical dissection in the Renaissance period, noting that even in relation to bodies, scientific 'fact' can only be seen through our cultural lens.[2]

Today, even sex as a binary is being challenged. Dupré suggests the advances of modern biology over the last half century render the dichotomous sexing of children as male or female no longer biologically defensible (2021, pp. 57). His description of the genome, not as something static and fixed, but as a 'dynamic participant, sensitive to a range of external influences' (2021, p. 71), means that sex and gender are not inscribed in the genes, or inevitable, but that male and female point to 'the most common developmental trajectories, but trajectories from which many individuals diverge' (p. 75). Indeed, some countries

---

2 During the Renaissance, up until the seventeenth century, dissection of female reproductive organs did not reveal a vagina and uterus, but what scientists saw, through the lens of their belief in a one sex body, was an inverted penis and a scrotum. Thus, Laqueur notes, seeing may be believing, but believing is also seeing (1992, pp. 79, 63–113).

(Germany, Australia, New Zealand) have now enabled babies to be registered at birth as of indeterminate sex.

Was the binary ever fully accurate, however? Helen King (2024) gives us many examples of bodies that have not, historically, conformed to a strict male or female sex: those born with both male and female sex organs present, women born without a womb, men who have been able to breastfeed, or menstruate and so on. The biological category of 'intersex', which has been present for some time but only recently removed from the shadows into public discourse, also challenges the idea of sex as a clear-cut binary. Today this attracts the diagnostic label of 'differences of sexual development' (DSD: a step up from 'a disorder of sexual development' DSM-5), or 'variations of sexual development' (VSD). We are thus on a journey to rethink whether sex itself can usefully be thought of as a clear binary.

For much of our history, including classical Greece and Rome, as well as in Judaeo-Christian antiquity, we might also note that *man* was considered to be the only sex. *Woman* was held to be at the imperfect end of a spectrum of difference held within this one sex. Thomas Laqueur (1992, p. 8) and others have written about the 'one-sex model', and contrasted it with the 'two-sex model', in which, the sexes can be seen as so separate as to be opposite. He suggests that the transition from a 'one-sex' to a 'two-sex' model took place in the eighteenth century, but Helen King (2013, 2024) suggests greater historical complexity.

In short, historically and in the current moment, our understanding of male and female sex as clearly binary can be questioned.

At this point, let us consider a little more how gender relates to sex.

The inter-relation of gender and sex

Judith Butler attributes the introduction of the concept of 'gender' to John Money, the sexologist who established it within medical scholarship in the late 1950s, with the aim of identifying and correcting people who were 'intersex' (2021, p. 27). Ideas about gender were thus an impetus to correct physical sex differences that did not conform to the male/female binary. In the 1970s, the diagnosis 'gender dysphoria' emerged, to describe a sense of gender and sex being out of sync for some people, and surgery became an option for adults to medically transition to match a person's internal sense of gender identity.

Foucault explores this idea of a 'true sex' emerging at odds with that shown by the body and problematizes the entire notion of a 'true sex' waiting to be discovered (Barbin, 1980, pp. xiii, vii–xvii), questioning the narrative that assumes there is one 'true' way to be, involving a unity of sex and gender. This kind of destabilizing is also favoured by John Dupré, who reports that those countries enabling babies to be registered as indeterminate sex are open to the charge that this only serves to maintain a fixed and determinative set of categories (2021, p. 63). He suggests that, instead of constructing ways of holding or identifying our bodies that are about 'capture, fixing, stilling', we abandon our commitment to 'colonial knowing' and move in an opposite direction to 'bewilderment', 'wildness' and openness (2021, pp. 40, 46–7).

I suggest that this is a helpful way to explore gender and sex in our current times, and as an illustration offer a conversation I had with a young person from Generation Z.[3] Teddy, assigned female at birth, identifies as a non-binary man and uses he/they pronouns. They cannot, for health reasons, choose medical interventions to make their body match their inner sense of self, and are therefore frequently identified as a woman. Acknowledging their body is 'an icon of a different thing', they suggested that they want 'to live in a fluid, queer space', to 'do the most chaotic thing' and 'whatever brings me the most joy'. Truth for Teddy is thus living with contradiction and making it creative, meaningful, joyful.

Teddy is perhaps an illustration, too, of Judith Butler's suggestion that everyone is 'searching for livable lives within the language that they find or make or refuse' (2021, p. 32). A binary discourse around gender is one that suits some individuals perfectly, and some regimes or narratives (including the patri-

---

3 The conversation took place on 25 June 2024 and is reproduced with permission.

archal narrative), but that does not suit others at all. Those who benefit from existing classifications experience their embodiments as 'right' and inevitable, but those who feel 'wrong', as Jack Halberstam notes, 'are made to feel so in relation to matrices of power and definition' (2021, p. 38).

Scripture

What does Scripture have to offer to this debate? In Genesis, we see two accounts of creation. In the first account (Genesis 1.27), we find both male and female are created simultaneously in God's image. In Genesis 2.21–22, woman is created from a rib taken from man, to be his helper. What do we make of these?

First, we could note that in Genesis 1, male *and* female are created in the image of God. In Genesis 2, we could also follow scholarship (including Goldingay, 2010, pp. 40–1, and Margaret Mowczko, 2013) that suggests that the 'man', *'ha'adam'* (הָאָדָם) can be more properly translated as 'the human', out of which both male and female, and arguably everything in between, exists. We could also propose that Genesis 2 supports the one-sex model and Genesis 1 the two-sex model, and that having both models available queers our understanding of one interpretation fits all. The writers of Genesis[4] had neither of these models in mind. The Genesis creation stories are not informed by modern conceptions of the body. Yet, as Paul Tillich (1967) recognized, each generation needs to interpret Scripture anew in order to answer the questions posed by our contemporary preoccupations. These are, I suggest, increasingly leading us in the direction of 'wildness'.

The Hebrews conceived creation as emerging out of chaos. God acts on chaos, but perhaps human beings need to tidy it up, an idea developed with tremendous force, imagination and scholarship by Catherine Keller (2003). Perhaps we should allow more of Keller's theology of *becoming* to influence our thinking,

---

4 According to the documentary hypothesis, P (the Priestly source) wrote Genesis 1 and J (the Yahwist), Genesis 2 (Von Rad, 1972, pp. 47, 73). Blenkinsopp challenges the idea that Genesis 2 is significantly older (Barton and Muddiman, 2104, p. 43).

to eschew the tidying into binaries so favoured of the 'separative work of the dominological order' (Keller, 2003, p. 99). She finds in the Spirit brooding on the waters at the beginning of creation (Genesis 1.2) 'the lost treasure, the pearl of great value' (p. 99). Perhaps we need to let this understanding of God's creative work infiltrate our interpretation of male and female. This would connect with Dupré's favouring of wildness and bewildering, and Teddy's story of making sense of a chaotic body.

This returns us to the question of God beyond gender. God has been seen in our doctrine as beyond sex, but this has not prevented us from attributing gender to God: male gender. Or we might say, in our theology and liturgy we have returned through our language and concepts to a one-sex model, where male is at the top, representing perfection. Is this really where we want to be?

The current destabilizing of binary sex and gender, and the favouring of a spectrum, we might say, is also offering a one-sex model. In the modern iteration, this is wilder, more dynamic and fluid: rather bewildering, indeed. If we persist in stilling and fixing God in a male perfection, whether in a one-sex or two-sex model, we are merely worshipping patriarchy, culture, our longing for certainty, fixture, arrival. Why not worship instead the unseen, bewildering, marvellously uncontrollable God, the God of becoming, of the depths, described by Keller? I suggest that the current wilding of gender can assist us with this. Or, to put it another way, at the very least this can help us to understand our current moment in relation to gender and sex through Scripture and tradition.[5]

Patriarchy

The simplest explanation of 'patriarchy' is etymological: from the Greek πατήρ/πατρός (*patēr/patros*) and ἀρχή (*archē*), *patriarchy* means the rule of the fathers (Johnson, 2002, pp. 23–4). It

---

5 Although I am excited by the possibilities of *wilding* our thinking about sex and gender, it is worth emphasizing that it is not necessary to share these views to make use of and benefit from the inclusive liturgy in this book.

describes a social and political system in which men govern. This covers institutions, norms, attitudes, language and more. Natalie Watson (2003, pp. 26–7) describes it as involving 'inherent gender bias': 'Patriarchy constructs a social-symbolic order in which men dominate women and women are viewed as the Other.' It is, she continues, 'a system, a web of relationships and institutions that … arranges the whole of life … in a hierarchical way. Patriarchal interests within theology and praxis have rendered women invisible in both church and theology' (pp. 26–7).

However, isn't 'patriarchy' a throwback to a previous wave of feminism? Kate Manne is sceptical about the tendency to categorize feminism in 'waves', as if there is an inbuilt obsolescence in feminist thinking, rather than the kind of amendment addition and growth that comes with other political discourse (2019, p. xxi). Nonetheless, research in 'gender studies' today tends to eschew patriarchy per se in favour of an emphasis on the complexity of power with its intersecting dimensions.

Feminists are, however, already acknowledging this intersectionality and diversity. Natalie Watson (2003, p. 27) suggests patriarchy is

> the name given to a web of systems which have developed in human history in which *some* male experience is made normative and most of the power to define and order reality is placed in the hands of men who are required to embody a particular construction of masculinity.

Kate Manne also notes that it is white, heterosexual, middle-class and non-disabled men who benefit most, subject to fewer constraints on their actions than their less privileged counterparts. Not all will, she continues, wish to take advantage of the tacit social permissions afforded by patriarchy (2019, p. xiii).

It is important to recognize diversity, intersectionality, individuality. Yet, the presence of the entitlements conveyed by patriarchy, which Manne details so well, and the way, indeed, in which the world is so often set up for women, comprehensively exposed by Caroline Criado-Perez (2019), render this concept still vital. Its vitality is partly demonstrated by a popular resurgence in its use. Feminism is currently characterized by online connectivity and global reach, as demonstrated by the #MeToo movement where there is a global reach to the readiness to reclaim patriarchy as a valid description of reality. While this does not mean we can use it uncritically, this book, in line with 'strategic essentialism', examines the ways in which gender justice and equality are constrained by existing power structures and norms and the continuing persistence of patterns that favour men, as outlined above.

As Neil Paynter put it,

> For me we would be post-patriarchy when we teach, preach and pray moving between masculine and feminine pronouns and images – without comment, without people saying, 'I can see you need it', or 'I think of God as love', who then see no inconsistency in saying 'Lord', 'he', etc. (2002, Month 4, Day 9, 'Women')

Liturgy

Liturgy comprises the words, actions and images that make up an act of worship. The term comes from the Greek words *laos*, meaning 'people', and *ergos*, meaning 'work', and is thus often understood as 'the work of the people'. This illustrates an important central tenet: it is not something given or imposed from above, but properly something that the people do together. Liturgy expresses doctrine, but also incorporates emotions, the body, our whole person, to stimulate the experience of being in the presence of a loving God. As Ian Tarrant suggests (2012, p. 4), it facilitates 'a life-changing interaction with God', but also expresses who we are as a worshipping congregation, strengthening 'both our community and our identity as members of the body of Christ'.

At its heart is corporate prayer, not just praying in words but also praying through the body, with music, art, silence, in a comprehensive, communal approach to God. In doing this, 'we offer ourselves to be shaped by the gospel we long to share', as Janet Morley suggests, and it 'gathers us together to be shaped as communities that seek to live out that gospel' (Morley, 1992,

p. 1). It thus becomes a shared activity and goal as well as 'a crucial form of action for change'. In calling on and naming God, we are 'explicitly naming and binding ourselves to what we most value', setting aside the values of our society and culture that we are 'unwittingly soaked in' and unthinkingly worship (Morley, 1992, p. 5) and leaving space for God to enter with a new thought, a new space, a sacred space. Indeed, if we are to somehow transcend our cultural context, even momentarily, it is surely by the grace and revelation of God, whose gospel can cause us to critique culture, whose living Word can indeed create an opportunity for something new.[6]

I give the last word to the Preface to the Church of Scotland *Book of Common Order*, which suggests that in liturgy 'our theology is formed, our discipleship encouraged, and our spirits nourished. It is in worship that we reach out to touch the hem of Christ's garment' and find 'we are being offered the grace of God' (1994, p. ix).

Inclusive

There are all kinds of ways worship can be inclusive. One can look at one's congregation and ponder if everyone there is feeling addressed and valued equally. This can relate to gender, but also to race, ethnicity, sexuality, ability, class, age, and more. Another valuable approach is to look at the congregation and ask, 'Who is not here?' And then wonder, 'Why?'

Being inclusive can mean ensuring the building is accessible to wheelchair users, that there is a hearing loop for those who need it, that guide dogs for people with sight loss are permitted, that large-print service sheets are available. It can relate to the images that are shown in church. Are they diverse or monochrome? It can relate to the parts of the Bible that are habitually shared. Do we hear the stories of women such as Judith or Esther or Hagar? How do we represent or address our congregation? Do we use

---

[6] This can be seen, for example, in the anti-slavery campaigns of the eighteenth and nineteenth centuries, where the gospel was an impetus to major cultural change.

people's correct pronouns? Are there gender-neutral toilets accessible to all? Are trans people ever mentioned? Are our social events middle class and exclusive? An inclusivity audit would be revealing for each of our churches.

This guide, however, focuses specifically on language and, more specifically, on our language for God. The inclusivity lens through which I consider this is that of gender. The question of how we approach God and what pronouns, images, titles we use are thus our direct concern.

3

Why? Why this Project and Why Me?

Language is powerful. Words matter to God, by whose word creation came into being. Through God, the Word was made flesh, and the Christ, present at creation, came among us to bring salvation. Language also matters to us, as human beings. We too create with it. We create relationships, with each other and with God. We describe and create our world with words. Sara Ahmed conveys this well by stating, 'words bring worlds with them' (2021, p. 245). They both convey and conduce a state of affairs. They are not neutral.

Language thus has the power to describe and distill our experiences and longings, but also the power to define and limit them. As Elizabeth Johnson puts it (2002, p. 27), 'language not only expresses the world but helps to shape and create it'. Language is the power to shape the world in our own image. Sherryl Kleinman concurs (2002, p. 300): 'Words are the tools of thought. We can use words to maintain the status quo or to think in new ways.' We can see this in the Bible: the prophets used their words to challenge the status quo, often targeting the readiness to take refuge in ritual sacrifice without true commitment to justice and care for the oppressed.

We too, in our liturgy, have taken refuge in the familiar, without considering what impact exclusively male language has on the women and girls who are using it. It has been asserted that using the generic male automatically includes women, but Caroline Criado-Perez has demonstrated conclusively how flawed this argument is and how directly the use of male language leads to imagining men in leadership roles and reducing options for women (2019, p. 5). Androcentric language has powerful consequences.

The danger of using exclusively male language for God is that it not only legitimates but adds sacred power to social systems of domination and patriarchy, proclaiming it 'ordained by God' (Schüssler Fiorenza, 1996, p. 171). Vivienne Faull and Jane Sinclair recount a five-year-old boy arguing that boys were better than girls who, when asked why, answered, 'Because God is a boy, isn't he?' (1986, pp. 2–21, also pp. 5–6; see also Read, 2024, p. 3). Having access to the divine mediated by maleness can create a sense of superiority in men and boys and undermine women and girls' sense of personhood and agency, leading them to 'an internalized sense of powerlessness' and low self-esteem (Johnson, 2002, p. 27), and to an increased dependence on men (Daly, 1985, p. 161). It can also lead to girls internalizing 'alienation and anger' and assuming the problem is with them, a situation that may well, as Schüssler Fiorenza suggests (1996, p. 169), warrant Bourdieu's designation of 'symbolic violence'.

This challenges us to look beyond the patriarchal setting of Scripture to the great themes that course through it: of creation, justice, love and salvation. God created male and female in God's own image; we are repeatedly reminded by the prophets, and elsewhere, of God's thundering justice and concern for the oppressed, the outcast, the overlooked; Jesus called us to love our neighbours as ourselves, showing us in the parable of the good Samaritan that our neighbour may be 'other' (Luke 10.25–37) – and gender is just one of many ways we 'other' one other. St Paul reminds us that we are all one 'in Christ', with no distinction (for example, Galatians 3.28), that salvation through faith admits of no hierarchy.

Changing our language has a missional as well as an ethical dimension. The patriarchal packaging of our Christian message is at odds with the secular emphasis on diversity and inclusion in the West, and the growing appetite for liberation; it makes the Church appear irrelevant to our ethical young people. It resides within a cultural milieu that is no longer supported. As such, it has become an occasion of sin.[1]

---

[1] An external circumstance that of its nature (or because of human nature) incites sin. The sin in this case is the limitation of women's flourishing.

Finally, what does this language do to our relationship with God? Sallie McFague (1982, p. 41), drawing on experts on language and metaphor, analyses the way in which the symbol of God the Father has become ossified, no longer pointing to the divine but fused with its literal meaning, such that it becomes an obstacle to faith, an idol, rather than an enabler, a point also made by Elizabeth Johnson (1997, p. 39) and Graham Adams (2024, pp. xi–xii). Mark Earey, one of the architects of *Common Worship*, and Phillip Tovey (2009, pp. 22, 24) also suggest that using the resources too rigidly 'can, in turn, form a static view of God'. They suggest, 'We may need to prune away some of the dead symbols.'

Scripture teaches us to treat each other with justice and integrity, to remove obstacles to faith in others, and to worship a God who is beyond any human category or limitation and who loves us all. Our liturgical language should demonstrate our commitment to these principles.

Why am I doing this?

One of the reasons I was drawn to Christianity, after a period of rebellious atheism, was the way Jesus treated women. He didn't patronize or sideline or exclude them, but talked with them, listened to them, treated them equally, encouraged them – like the men – to put aside what they were doing and listen to him; in other words, he treated them as disciples. The first person to whom the resurrected Christ appeared was a woman. He sent her to the apostles to deliver the good news. You might say Jesus exemplified a *kenosis* of the ruling male understanding of masculinity. This spoke powerfully to me as a woman in a patriarchal society. Yet, on my path to ordination, I encountered resiliently male language in our liturgy, and even when ordained I was aware that to challenge or problematize this male language was taboo.

When I wrote or received liturgy that did not do this, which was creative, inclusive, shocking (creating a service with a female Christa springs to mind), it had a visceral effect on me. I was powerfully moved. When attending such services, I felt seen, valued. More than this, I felt broken open. Into this raw, tender opening I found myself filled – with emotion, gratitude, recognition, with the Holy Spirit. Like Mary, I felt commissioned.

I am now the lead for inclusive liturgy on the WATCH Executive Committee, which gives me a platform to deliver inclusive liturgy nationally. When I do so, I find women weep and are deeply moved; they thank me effusively. It is for this reason I continue.

WATCH has for some time sought to produce a guide that would empower women to write and use their own inclusive liturgy. I took this on, and it grew. I began by simply including female images for God, to accompany and refresh our overwhelmingly male language, and this developed into greater inclusivity. Perhaps inclusivity work is like this – you are aware of where exclusion impacts you, but when you begin to address it, you realize it's a lot larger than your individual starting point, with reverberations beyond into other marginalized peoples.

4

Principles and Practicals

In this chapter, I shall look at some of the practical steps that can usefully be taken before introducing inclusive liturgy, as well as how to successfully introduce it.

Self-assessment

The beginning of crafting inclusive liturgy is to assess your current context, the reality in which you find yourself. What language is currently used in your church? Do your words conjure ruling and submission and convey patriarchally male aspects of God? Do you pray to God as Almighty Father, all-powerful, Lord and King? Do you always refer to God as 'he'? What impact might this be having? Janet Morley (1992, p. 6) notes that by unthinkingly using this language habitually, we are in danger of blessing worldly systems of power that 'impoverish and endanger those with least power over their own lives'. Have you thought sufficiently about the power inherent in your habitual language for God?

What would it be like to use alternative images of God, as tender, vulnerable, alongside us, as playful, sister, sustainer, child? What would it be like to pray, 'Wake up / little baby God'?[1] In Scripture, God is delighting, cooperating, rock, fire, wind. Sallie McFague suggests God as mother, lover and friend (1989, p. xi), images that may seem new and arresting, yet are also based in tradition. Such variation can stimulate us to wonder and a fresh relating to God.

---

1 A prayer in a Chilean Christmas card quoted by Janet Morley (1992, p. 44).

Purpose

If you decide to inclusivize your liturgy, it is important to be clear about purpose.

Your purpose

Is this a question of justice for you, of righting a wrong, of including the excluded? Women occupy the pews of churches, yet both lay and ordained women find their worship refracted through language that privileges men and maleness in God and welcomes women as secondary, as valued companions, rather than in their own right. Perhaps you feel that this needs to be addressed. What about those whose gender is non-binary or who are transitioning or who do not conform to traditional gender identifications – are they welcome? As Alex Clare-Young points out (2024), accurate mirroring for genderqueer people is essential to facilitate a sense of full personhood. All of us, whatever gender, are created in the image of God, yet God is beyond each one of us. If we use images that are not simply a representation of ourselves, it helps remind all of us that God is beyond us, not just the senior member of a club of people like us.

What other purpose or incentive might you have? Perhaps you are addressing a need, a wish, that has been expressed to you by a member of the congregation and you want to respond to that challenge with love.

Your purpose may be pastoral. For those who have been damaged or abused by men, a powerfully male God may be alienating; they may, instead, need to feel that God understands their vulnerability and you want to address that, even if it has not been expressed openly.

Or you may wish to do something exploratory to refresh your worship, not fully sure of where it will lead or what it might mean.

Whatever your purpose, it is important that it is steeped in love, that you care about people's growth, the effect the worship has on them, the speed they can move at, their blockages and their freedoms, their longings and needs. Only then will your liturgy have any hope of meeting them, drawing them forward.

Be aware that you are treading on sacred ground and that you may find it in some surprising places.

The purpose of the worship

Who is the worship for? A group of like-minded people, who long to be fed? The merely curious? The full congregation? Who are your congregation – do you know, or have you made gendered and heteronormative assumptions? Whom might you have rendered invisible by not remaining open, curious or exploring, asking questions?

Is your intention to educate and inspire, challenge and stimulate, or comfort and sooth? Are you seeking to provide a quiet contemplative atmosphere or a lively, uplifting one?

Is it in a particular season – a call to repentance in Lent, or the celebration of Easter, for example? If you are Anglican, it is significant to note whether your liturgy is for the Principal Service on a Sunday. This has different requirements to a midweek or second Sunday service (see the Appendix).

Your choice of language needs to suit your intention and audience.

Planning

Be clear about the reality of your context. If your people are longing for this kind of service or willing to be gently led, you may wish simply to begin normalizing female imagery and see how people respond.

If change is likely to be resisted, more planning is needed. Involve your stakeholders. Explain your theological reasons and hopes. Be inspiring. Be biblical: 'Behold I will do a new thing' (Isaiah 43.19, KJV). Mine the resources of Scripture and tradition to find female images of God, or male images that defy stereotypes, or a combination. (Think of Isaiah 42.13–14 where God is both a warrior and a woman in labour in successive verses.) Seek out examples of feminist liturgy and prayer. One such is Nicola Slee's *Praying Like a Woman* (2024), which contains examples of feminist prayer and liturgy. Other resources are listed in Chapter

8, References and Resources. Or, begin to experiment with writing your own material, accessing WATCH liturgy-writing events for support (details on the WATCH website).[2] Identify allies, who can be leaven in the dough, encouraging others. Get the backing of your governing body, Parochial Church Council or Council of Elders, for example, if it is likely to be controversial. Take the time that is necessary to prepare the way.

In the Anglican parish where I was a curate, we often sang 'These are the days of Elijah', honouring the patriarchs, in our informal 'fresh expression' service. I replaced this, without explanation, with 'These are the days of Rebekah', which substitutes notable women from the Bible (such as Rebekah and Esther) and found that it provoked annoyance and rejection. However, when I used it again in the context of a sermon series on *women*, and explained my reasons, it was much more positively received. The music group later developed a version with both women and men, accepting the principle but remaining uncomfortable with domination by what they saw as 'either' gender.

This vignette shows the value of explaining what you are doing and why, and of both understanding and respecting your context – where people are, and the way in which they are comfortable incorporating new material and emphases. You may find them more receptive to achieving balance in the here and now, rather than wishing to redress the historical imbalance by including a preponderance of excluded images. If you long to worship God without any male images, you might find this is best kept for a group of like-minded people, at least in the first instance. Also, don't forget that thinking in binary terms leaves those who do not identify in these terms unrepresented.

It is important to review and honour people's responses. This will help you assess if you have judged your people's readiness for change correctly. When planning a new service, provide space afterwards, over coffee perhaps, to talk about it: what felt fresh and exciting, what disturbed, what would people be willing to try again, what was a step too far? Manage the discussion, with clear ground rules on confidentiality, mutual respect and listening. This will assist people in digesting something new. This could

---

2 https://www.womenandthechurch.org (accessed 8.7.2025).

prompt further discussion about who else our language excludes and stimulate a group to plan another service together. You could also discover new things about each other in the process, in terms of identity, theology and openness to change. This was certainly my experience after curating a group to pray with, then discuss, Julian of Norwich's ideas around 'Christ our Mother'. You may, as I did, find the conversation enlivening, even exhilarating.

Exploring identity

Be aware that you may have made assumptions about others' gender identity that are incorrect. Be open to learning. If you are a homogenous group, think about why that is and consider inviting others in, to offer hospitality and learn from them. Be gentle, for you are treading on sacred ground. Be kind. Be aware that we are all individuals and everyone with a particular gender designation will not necessarily think or feel the same way.

If you are in a church of Black Christians, you may find that people in this context consider changing gendered terms for God to be a white or European phenomenon. I speak here as a white (Northern Irish) Christian, who has had conversations with Black Christians in which this has been highlighted. To include Black Christians in a mixed church, it may be more important to emphasize themes of justice, God on the side of the oppressed, God as beyond gender, rather than presenting a specific gender or pronoun. Jennifer Thomas, a member of WATCH's Executive Committee, told me, 'From my perspective our view of God is in your lived experience and your relationship.'[3] Don't make assumptions. Ask people.

For some within the trans community, feminists who insist on retaining 'woman' and 'she' as markers are failing to include the complexity of their experience. This is where intersectionality gets tricky, as Naomi Nixon, another Executive Committee member of WATCH and Chief Executive Officer at the Student Christian Movement put it.[4] Explaining why she advocates

---

3 This was in a virtual online conversation (30 July 2024) about how to make worship inclusive of Black women.
4 Virtual online conversation, 11 July 2024.

for adding non-binary terms, rather than simply using them for everyone, she seeks to explain that giving up specifically female imagery and terminology isn't giving up a privilege but 'a hard-won being seen, which is only just being won'. This self-identification as *women* remains central to women who are still fighting to be visible in Western society. Wrestling with these tensions is important and, following Naomi, I suggest we retain 'woman' and 'she', but alongside this, embrace wisdom from those who identify as non-binary and those who are transitioning or genderqueer. This reminds us to avoid gender stereotypes, to include non-gendered images, and to enable our images of God to embrace all genders and none. However, we probably can't do everything all at once. Once again, knowing where your people are and where they might be willing to be led in the first instance is a good guide.

Exploring theology

Does your theology embrace change, transition, continuing createdness, complexity? Do you value curiosity, exploration? These are themes that sit well with the trans community. In my conversation with Teddy (see p. 12), they spoke to me of a nun at their school who declared, 'God didn't create the world finished, God didn't create anyone finished, it's up to you to finish yourself.' How does that sit with your view of God? Is it worth beginning by having a conversation with yourself and with others about how you view God or want to represent God in your setting? Think about whether a vulnerable God could speak to those who feel vulnerable, what it would be like to set this image alongside images of power, just as God set aside power in incarnating as a baby. Think about whether or how you are presenting God as a God of justice, on the side of the marginalized, and whether you need to expand your understanding of that.

Also think about your anthropology, in particular about sin, how you envisage it. Is sin gendered? One (essentialist) feminist approach suggests that the preoccupation with pride as the besetting human sin does not reflect female experience. For women, the argument goes, the sin that is more seductive is that of not feeling one is enough, of tending to value oneself as less than, rather than too much.⁵ This has implications for how one writes confessions. What are we sorry for? What do we need to repent of? We begin our services by repenting of our sins, and this is an opportunity to consider how we are presenting this aspect of being human.

It's not just about words ...

Silence

As Janet Morley notes, 'Space and silence should be included as an integral part of worship' (1992, p. 7), as packing a service with too many unfamiliar words may be overwhelming. Music and silence both give pauses in which to absorb the vivid images that have been offered, the unfamiliar territory that has been traversed.

Music

Music is a key part of liturgy. Songs and hymns express our doctrine, our theology, our faith, and enable us to sing, to take part in the work of the people and to raise our spirits to God. So often the lyrics we sing are resolutely patriarchal. There are resources available, however, which do something new (see References and Resources). One approach is to take familiar tunes and write new lyrics for them. John Bell and Graham Maule (2018) have done this in *Known Unknowns*, and Ally Barrett has a body of work that can be sung to well-known tunes. Another approach is to take known words and make them feel very different by changing the musical form, as Siskin Green have done, notably with 'Will your anchor hold?' and 'For those in peril'. Here, they take traditional hymns, beloved of the Boy's Brigade and the Royal Navy, respectively, and subvert them by a folk setting. 'Will your anchor hold?', transformed from its 'bold, declamatory' tenor to a 'minor bluegrass Appalachian picking

---

5 See Watson, 2003, pp. 40–2, for a summary of feminist discourses of sin and salvation.

thing', truly, as Jonathan Langley notes (2024, p.20), becomes a question. In their version of the nineteenth-century hymn by Anna Waring, 'Heart full of anxious request', the band also uses female pronouns for God, calls on 'my Mother in heaven' who makes us 'pure by the blood that She shed'. Female blood, as Jonathan Langley notices (2024, p. 19), has a very different connotation to male blood. Here, a combination of lyric adaptation and setting make for a very different experience.

Art

Images can be chosen to support the inclusive words. Abstract, allusive images can work particularly well in my experience. In online liturgy this is especially important and can be a potent support to opening up our vision of the God we approach. The images can provide an extra dimension of beauty as well as illustration. The same caution is needed as with too many unfamiliar words – the combination of unfamiliar, vibrant images and words can require a quieter period in which to rest, process, consolidate.

Pitfalls and possibilities

Speed of change

Going too slowly or too fast are both potential pitfalls, depending on your context, so plan and pray first.

Familiarity

Familiarity is important in worship, so find a balance between the innovative and that which has long forged a path to the divine in people's hearts and minds.

Be aware of others' red lines, that beyond which they cannot comfortably move. The Lord's Prayer is, for many, a prayer that should not be changed. I shall now consider this prayer in some detail, as I believe there is more room for movement here than may be generally understood.

The Lord's Prayer

Writing this prayer in one's own words is a long-established spiritual practice, as shown by Bishop Kenneth Stevenson (2004). There are two Bible versions (Luke 11.1–4 and Matthew 6.9–13), as noted both by Stevenson and Nicola Slee (2022, p. 9), each with differences oriented to the Gospel writers' audiences. The words have also been changed across time: the Anglo-Saxon 'forgyf us ure gyltas' became forgive our 'debtors' in the Scottish Reformation version, whereas the 1549 English Prayer Book forgives 'trespassers'. There is also the context of place: the Church of the Pater Noster on the Mount of Olives displays the prayer in 140 languages. Everyone regards their own language as authentic.

Janet Morley notes the choice we are presented with on whether the 'daily bread' petition is asking for 'strength to keep going' in today's world or 'the Messianic feast for the poor that is a sign of a totally different world order'. She also notes that those who are not actually hungry for bread make this a prayer for 'spiritual stamina', whereas 'Christians in the poorest parts of our world pray quite differently. They pray for real food, but they are also hungry for justice' (1992, p. 2).

We might also consider the 'liberties' taken by key figures in our church tradition. Archbishop William Laud paraphrased the Lord's Prayer as a devotional exercise. Leonardo Boff, a leading proponent of liberation theology, focused on just one of the petitions, 'thy Kingdom come', which he interpreted as liberation from earthly oppression. Teresa de Avila contemplated each petition for an hour.

These responses lead Bishop Stevenson to suggest that the Lord's Prayer is 'less ... a formula to be recited ... more ... a light shining from a distance on an ongoing discipleship'. It is, he suggests, 'a living text, whose narrative is constantly being written' (2004, pp. 53, 175, 31–3) a situation also noted by Slee, who suggests 'variation in the text of the Lord's Prayer is there from its very beginning, built into its warp and weft' (2022, p. 9).

Teaching on this would assist and writing one's own Lord's Prayer could become a spiritual exercise. The prayers could then be discussed, displayed, prayed, honoured.

Alternatively, one group could recite the traditional words and another an inclusive language version. This way, what is perceived as the 'original' prayer is retained. One can also invite people to recite the prayer in the language/words of their choice. This opens up the possibility of other languages as well as other English words.

Images of God

There are a number of options when we are aiming to be both gender-less and gender-full. The first step is to consider whether you want to use gender neutral language, or whether you wish to incorporate specifically female images, or whether you want to include images that represent the complexity of gender inclusion. Don't assume you can do all of it at once. Where can you start? What is realistic and will help people to travel with you?

Female images

The Creator as Mother offers a powerful connection to birth and nurturing, perhaps best accessed, as Sallie McFague suggests (1996, p. 325), by the emphasis on the tasks of motherhood: giving birth, feeding and protecting the young, longing for their flourishing. This has implications for God's closeness to us – held in God's womb, rather than created as a potter uses clay – as well as for creation, if we envisage the Creator as birthing the world. It thus impacts our theology.

A pitfall is that it simply produces a new hierarchical dualism. Replacing God the Father with God the Mother would have the same difficulties as using one metaphor literally and exclusively, whereby the metaphor's lively connection to the divine ossifies (see Sallie McFague, 1982). The image of God as Mother can also exclude women who are not mothers and alienate those who have had negative experiences of mother, just as those with abusive, absent or otherwise difficult fathers can find God the Father unhelpful. We should also note that people identifying as non-binary would be more included by Parent than Mother or Father.

We need also to bear in mind that portraying God exclusively as parent/mother/father can also be infantilizing, deterring us from taking appropriate responsibility for our own growth and the well-being of our planet (McFague 1996, p. 325). Graham Adam's book, *God the Child* (2024), is a good exposition of the benefits of taking a child's-eye view, which of course occurred in the birth of Jesus.

Sentimentalizing and stereotyping maternal imagery is another danger. Thus, 'mother' becomes associated with nurture, while power remains male. This renders 'mother' merely another tool of oppression, a point developed by McFague (1996).

One solution is to combine tenderness with fierceness. An image I used of God as 'tiger-fierce' was considered powerful and liberating by some – women could relate to the fierceness of a tiger protecting her cubs. Using female pronouns or roles with qualities traditionally associated with maleness, and vice versa, helps to remind us of the complexity of God and also of our own complexity, powerfully and richly made by that same God.

Moving to the second person of the Trinity, here, one might say, we are in inarguably male territory. One response to this is to focus on how Jesus challenged the patriarchal representation of maleness as involving power-over. Another is to de-emphasize gender as no more significant than Jewishness, age or 'class'. A third is to emphasize the gender-neutral significance of the Christ (as opposed to the maleness of Jesus the man).[6] Alex Clare-Young suggests (2024,), 'Jesus as masculine-presenting was freed or stretched at Pentecost and resurrection to become the gender full Christ' who could 'encompass everything'. Developing this, if Christ, present from creation, is not a man but the God of classical theology, beyond gender, then Christ can be represented by the female as well as the male. *Christa*, a sculpture of a female figure on a cross, controversially displayed in New York in 1984 and again in 2016, demonstrates this approach. This is another potent area, where what is gained in understanding needs to be assessed against the offence that may be caused to some.

---

6 See Watson, 2003, pp. 33–7, for an exposition of feminist responses to the maleness of Christ.

The Hebrew word for Spirit, the *ruach*, is female in gender. Thus, another approach is to refer to the Holy Spirit as 'she', and the remainder of God as 'he'. This compartmentalizes femaleness in one person of the Trinity, but at least introduces people to the idea of God as 'she' in a contained way.

I suggest it is better to allow the female to stand for the whole of God and the whole of humanity, as male language and images have been used. Instead of associating femaleness with stereotypically nurturing qualities and aspects of God, and male with powerful and ruling qualities, allow both female and male to represent the full gamut of qualities that we attribute to God.

Pronouns

The question of pronouns is a potent one. Male pronouns are normative and change in this area can be shocking to people because it can seem to subvert the God they have always worshipped, identified as 'Lord', 'Father', 'He'. This might lead to the question, is this still the same God? Identifying God by the female pronoun has long been excluded: it was associated with fertility cults when YHWH was revealed to the Children of Israel, assimilated into a patriarchal culture, and then overlaid by centuries of patriarchal reception. This has rendered the use of 'she' taboo. One 'she' will carry a great deal of weight and be unmistakable, so if you want to arrest, call to attention, use 'she'. Bear in mind that using biblical motherly images may be more acceptable to people accommodating slowly to change than the use of the 'she' pronoun.

For those who are non-binary, the use of 'they/them' will enable them to feel mirrored and included, that they have been seen, that God is not alien to them, but loves them in their humanity. The theological objection here is that this takes us away from monotheism. Against this, we may note that the *Oxford English Dictionary* now accepts 'they' as a singular pronoun. Additionally, we worship God as a Trinitarian community, so an alternative argument is that the use of 'they' reminds us of this complexity, by its capacity to represent both singular and plural.

In the Church of Scotland *Book of Common Order*, pronouns are placed in italics. This is another possibility, as it draws attention to the provisionality of the pronoun and could also be interpreted as an opportunity to insert the pronoun that most helps you to approach God. This could be useful in a congregation of mixed views.

Other less familiar pronouns that the trans community offer us include: ze/hir/hirs; xe/xem/xyrs; ve/vem/vir. These are known as 'neopronouns'. Per, ze, sie or ve can replace he or she, hir can replace him or her, and there are many other options. What would it be like to explore using entirely unfamiliar pronouns to express something of the otherness of God? Or, alternatively, if these are pronouns you are accustomed to using only in a select community, which in your experience have no traction in wider society, what would it be like to find something that is so personal to you included (publicly) in your approach to that which is arguably most personal of all, God?

Other ways of gentling people away from God as 'he' include the use of 'you', 'thou' or 'God' as a pronoun. Alternating male and female pronouns can usefully disrupt expectations, which is enlivening for some but for others distracts. Again, consider the purpose of your worship and those attending.

For some people, 'God' is so filled with negative projections and irredeemably male that they prefer to use an alternative term. Even for those who are not 'post-God' in this way, using alternative terms can be refreshing. These could include the Divine, the Holy or Holy of Holies, the Eternal, the Most High, the Numinous, Spirit, Creator, Holy (Wholly?) Other, Spirit of the Depths/Heights, Source. How do you wish to reference the divine?

I suggest that what is beneficial to the most people, and also thoroughly scriptural, is to have a range of images, epithets and pronouns available with which to approach God/the Holy.

PART 2

Putting it into Practice: Examples of Inclusive Liturgy

5

Examples and Resources: Getting Creative

This chapter gives short examples of inclusive liturgy for use within services. You can use them in their entirety, adapt them to your context, or let them serve as inspiration to write your own versions.

As context matters, I provide a short introductory note to describe the material in those cases where it was written for a particular group or season. As I am an Anglican priest, this material comes from an Anglican stable. One significant aspect of this context is that Canon Law regulates where one can write one's own material and where one is constrained to use authorized liturgy, whereas other Reformed Protestant denominations will find themselves freer. The Appendix provides guidelines for Anglicans on what creative licence is possible while remaining within the limitations of Canon Law. Anglican readers may find it encouraging, as much more is possible than is often realized.

However, as noted in the Introduction, I hope this material will be of use by many other Christian traditions and denominations. Christian services share broadly similar content, even if presented in a different order or with different emphases. We are all moved to praise God, to say sorry for our sins, and to pray for others.

Whatever denomination you are, I encourage you to mine these examples, use those that are useful and ignore those that are not.

CONFESSIONS AND ABSOLUTIONS

WATCH provides Inclusive Liturgy Writing Days, many of which I have led, and the following confessions and absolutions come from these days. For Anglicans attentive to Canon Law, please see the Appendix about the restrictions we face in this area. However, we can also note that Anglican tradition has often developed from the ground up. Thus, regularly doing something new on the ground can lead to change in regulations and stipulations, which recognizes and validates those places where the Spirit has already led the people.

When we write confessions and absolutions, we are impelled to ponder and clarify what it is we consider to be sin, what sin we find ourselves wanting to repent of in the context for which we write, and what kind of forgiveness we need. I find that I often return to the same themes and one of the challenges here is finding ways to keep our material fresh. Another approach is to choose or write one confession and then use it regularly. This will make it familiar, and familiarity, as I have noted above, can assist us in prayer, where the repetition becomes a kind of meditation, taking us beyond the words, which is where, ironically, in the end we wish to go.

Confession 1: Advent

We have waited in your bright darkness
And seen only death.

God who comes,
Forgive us.

We have hunkered down
When we could have grown.

God who comes,
Forgive us.

We have given way to fear
Instead of trusting to raw hope.

God who comes,
Forgive us.

Confession 2: Ordinary Time

Holy God,
We have squandered your gift of life,
Clinging to that which is passing,
Controlling that which should be free.

God, have mercy.
God, have mercy.

Vulnerable God,
We have turned from the Cross,
We have shunned suffering
And sought our ease.

Christ, have mercy.
Christ, have mercy.

Living God,
We have denied relationship
And closed down
When we could have opened.

God, have mercy.
God, have mercy.

Absolution

God of mercy and of love,
Forgive us all we have
Squandered,
Set aside and
Spoiled.
Set us free
To live as your friends
In the name of the one
Who lived on earth
As the friend of all.
Amen.

Confession 3: Lent

We have glimpsed
The promised land
And hidden in the shadows.

God, have mercy.
God, have mercy.

We have nestled
In the darkness
And spurned growth.

Christ, have mercy.
Christ, have mercy.

We have reduced
God's glorious kin-dom
To a promise
Which is ours alone.

God, have mercy.
God, have mercy.

Absolution

May the God
Who is greater than all we can imagine
Have mercy on us,
Pardon our offences
And break us into new life.
Amen.

COLLECTS

How to write a Collect

Collects are a regular part of Christian services and serve to gather up the prayers of the people. In the Anglican context, the Collect occurs in the Gathering, after the Confession, following a short silence, when it sets the intention of the service and gathers up the prayers before the move into the Liturgy of the Word (Earey, 2011, p. 40) or at the end of the prayers of intercession.

One way to approach writing a Collect is to treat it as if you are writing a poem. One common feature is the value of a structure. Collects are usually 8–12 lines long.

- They begin by naming God in a line or even one word followed by a comma, and then describe or evoke a quality or behaviour of God, or an aspect of God's story. This encourages worshippers to recognize a wider range of attributes of God. It is usually one to three lines and is followed by a colon.
- The next section contains the petition, the 'ask': 'help us to', 'may we so', 'grant that we' and so on, another two to three lines.
- Collects conclude by calling on God again, either Jesus or a full Trinitarian evocation, and the people assent: Amen.

Perhaps the most important thing to remember, rather than commas or colons is that the whole thing is designed to read as one, connected sentence.

As with a poem, the use of the symbolic is paramount. Choose words or an image that touches the heart, or gentles the soul, which breaks open a new feeling, or transforms the familiar into the revelatory.

How do you want to call on God? What aspect of God are you describing or evoking or worshipping, and how might you help extend our experience of God? The names in the authorized collects include 'Mighty God', 'Gracious God' and 'Everlasting God'. Steven Shakespeare opts for: 'Lord of fierce compassion', 'God of the outstretched hand', 'God of the wrong crowd' (2009, pp. 50–1). Janet Morley chooses: 'O God our disturber', 'Spirit of energy and change', 'O God, the source of all insight' (1992, pp. 5, 7). Lastly, Cole Arthur Riley's suggestions include: 'God of locked doors', 'God of the kitchen table', 'God our home', 'God of sacred darkness' (2024, pp. 28–30, 37).

Consider what help or transformation you need. More inclusive language, yes, but why, to what end? Delve into your hearts, find where you are thirsty and pray to have that thirst quenched. But make it corporate, connect it with others, with the community for whom you will pray. Where is their thirst? What is your thirst for them? What is God's thirst for them?

Collect for Advent

God who is here
And yet coming,
Beyond and yet within,
Melt the hard places
Of our hearts
With your audacious love.
Open our fear-locked doors
With your hope
And enable us to risk everything
With your daring.
In the name of the one
Who chose
The womb of Mary
To be born.
Amen.

Collects for Easter

Maundy Thursday

God our foot-washer,
Open us to your
Vulnerable presence,
Your tender love
And your eternal mercy

In the holy ground
Of our bodies,
Created and sustained by you.
In your holy name we pray.
Amen.

Good Friday

Broken God,
We bring our tears
For your brokenness,
For our brokenness,
And for the breaking we have done.
Help us
Like the women at the foot of the cross
Not to look away
But to wait with you.
In the name of our suffering Saviour
Who took all our brokenness into himself
And redeemed it.
Amen.

The next Collect was written during a WATCH writing day in the season of Lent, which had as its theme, Wilderness.

God of the wild places,
Unruly, fierce and free,
Smash the walls that imprison,
Break us out of the small places
In which we are content
And enable us to see new vistas,
Dream bold dreams,
Find our true selves.
We ask this in the name of
The God who calls us
Into her liberating darkness,
El-roi, the one who sees me.
Amen.

INTERCESSIONS AND OTHER PRAYERS

In the following prayer, 'forebears' can be substituted for 'foremothers'.

The list of activities in the second stanza can be varied to suit the people who are praying and the range of their activities, or made more specific for a shared purpose.

The Annunciation

God of our foremothers,
Teach us how to be like Mary.

Help us to be open,
Primed to encounter you in the everyday,
Listening,
Ready to absorb you
Through every cell in our bodies,
Even as we read or make tea,
or write,
or organize,
or lead or follow
in all the things we do in our everyday lives.

God of our foremothers,
Hear us.

Help us to be bold,
Ready to accept a challenge,
To do something unexpected,
To risk disapproval,
To move from the path we had envisaged for ourselves
Into your marvellous unexpectedness.

God of our foremothers,
Hear us.

Help us to give everything:
Our bodies, our souls,
Our comfort, our lives.

Make us pregnant with your Spirit
That our fullness may lead to
Complete, disruptive, overturning life.

God of our foremothers,
Hear us.

Merciful God,
Hear us as we pray to you,
Come to us as we listen for you,
And enter us with your living Word
That we may give birth to you again and again.
Amen.

Wilderness (Lent)

1 Prayer

God of the wilderness,
When we submit to
Busyness and clutter,
Strip us,
Give us bare land
And an empty landscape
Where we may find you.

Merciful God,
Hear our prayer.

God of the journey,
Be with us in our wandering,
Nourish us in our lack,
And reveal yourself to us
In our emptiness.

Merciful God,
Hear our prayer.

God of the lost and cast out,
When the world rejects us
Open us to your life-giving gaze,

The gaze that cherishes,
The love that never ceases.

Merciful God,
Hear our prayer,

Liberating God,
Accept these prayers
For the sake of your Son,
Who chose the desert
To embrace his true self.
Amen.

2 Prayer poem

Go before us, O God,
As you have been cloud and fire,
Discerning our needs
And meeting them
Through our long sojourn
In the wilderness.

> We thought it would never end
> But here we are
> Gazing out onto the promised land
> And wondering.

Go before us, O God,
As we leave this difficult terrain,
This sparseness
In which, yet, we have known you,
You with us, always with us,
And in which we have
Encountered ourselves
As if for the first time.

> Can we trust in the promise?
> Will the new land indeed be
> All that we hope for?
> Will our God stay with us?
> For a land of plenty

Without her
Is not the promise fulfilled.

And so we pray.

Go before us, O God,
As we leave this place
And enter the new landscape
Of milk and honey.
Be the pillar
We need in our new home.
Go before us
And remain with us,
Our source, our salvation, our joy.
Amen.

Advent

God who sees,
I have refused your vision of me,
Your glory in me,
And embraced the accuser's lies.
Help me to see as you see
And to love what you have made in me.

God who hears,
I have listened to another's voice,
Preferring the seduction of the lesser.
Hear my cry to you
That I may be fully yours.

God who knows,
Show me what it is
To walk in the light of truth,
To speak with the prophet's edge
And to dare the real.
Amen.

ALTERNATIVE LORD'S PRAYERS

One way to make these less controversial is simply not to call them Lord's Prayers. People will recognize the cadences even without the label. On the other hand, calling them Alternative Lord's Prayers draws attention to the spiritual freedom available through reimagining the words attributed to Jesus, embracing the intimacy and freedom that *his* reimagining captured, in words that speak to us in new ways.

I wrote my first of these in 2019, which I regard as my 'standard', and then wrote a number of others for different contexts. Further examples can be found in Chapter 6, within Services of the Word. This is the case for all the non-Eucharistic prayers in this section.

Alternative Lord's Prayer, 2019

Life-birthing God,
In whose love and hope is joy,
Let your wholiness[1] be known,
Your flourishing made manifest
Here on earth
As in all your creation.
Help us to find what we need
And not take more than we need,
Or what is not good for us,
Or what is not ours.
Help us to resist all that thwarts your purpose
And forgive us those times when we fail
To live your glorious vision,
As we forgive those who seek to quench
The life that is in us
And in those whom we love.

---

[1] A deliberate combination of wholeness and holiness. It will sound like 'holiness' but those reading the written word will be able to ponder another level of meaning.

For you alone are the centre, the beginning, and the end
Of all that is real, alive and good.
Amen.

Alternative Lord's Prayer, 2023

Inspired by the New Zealand Lord's Prayer[2]

Our Maker, in the holiness of eternity,
May your name be praised throughout our land,
Your vision bring us flourishing.
Help us to follow you, our Holy Guide,
That earth may resound with the wisdom of heaven.
Give us all we need to live
And forgive us when we move away from your path,
As we forgive those who wrong us.
Keep us from trials too great for us
And shield us from the enveloping darkness,
For yours is the power of love
Now and forever.
Amen.

---

2 At https://livinghour.org/lords-prayer/new-zealand-maori/ (accessed 04.04.2025).

PREFACES TO EUCHARISTIC PRAYER

How to write a Preface

Before the Eucharistic prayer, we may write either a short or extended preface, in which the creative and redemptive power of God is praised. Prefaces are followed by the Sanctus. It is a good idea to read existing examples and see how they proceed before writing your own. Think about the season you are in and which aspect of God you wish to single out for emphasis. Further notes for Anglicans (which may be useful for others) are available in the Appendix.

Eucharistic Preface 1 – Advent

God of the journey,
Who travels towards us and with us,
The I AM in whom our lives are set,
We praise and thank you
That you are on your way.
God of life, we praise you.

We open our hearts to the
Almost but not-yet,
We pledge our selves
To the fulfilment that beckons.
God of life, we praise you.

We rejoice in the eternal yes
That speaks itself in our hearts
As you come in vulnerable glory among us.
God of life we praise you.

Therefore, with angels and archangels
And with all the company of heaven
We proclaim your rich and risk-taking name,
I AM THAT I WILL BE,
Forever praising you and saying ...

Eucharistic Preface 2 – Wilderness (Lent)

It is our duty and our joy
To give thanks to you,
Ever-living God,
For you led us through the wilderness,
And in our darkness and uncertainty
Your steadfast presence guided and sustained us.
As we glimpsed an end to wandering
And wondered
You held us in our hoping,
And as we dance for joy
In this promised land
You, O God, are the dance
That moves in us and through us.
Therefore, with angels and archangels
And all the company of heaven
We proclaim your glory
Forever praising you and singing …

Eucharistic Preface 3 – Easter

In this holy week of Easter
It is indeed right
To praise you, Creator God,
You who made the earth
And all your creatures.
You who bring to birth,
Creating and making new
Yesterday, today and forever.

God our maker,
We praise your holy name.

You gave us Jesus
Born of a woman,
Friend of women,
Friend of the outcast,
Friend of us all,

Who showed us how to live,
Whom death could not contain.

God our friend,
We praise your holy name.

Holy God,
You breathed your holy essence
Upon us,
Within us,
Between us,
We are not alone.

God among us,
We praise your holy name.

And so we raise our voices
To join in the eternal song of heaven
In gratitude and joy.

Eucharistic Preface 4

Ever-giving, ever-loving God,
In all times and in all places
It is right to give you praise.
In Jesus your Son, our Saviour,
You came among us
As one born of Mary,
Whose friendship with the outcasts
Servant love and rigorous challenge
Taught us how to live,
In the paradox of a man
Born of woman and of God,
Whose suffering led to death
And in death birthed new life.
Open our hearts
To the mystery of your eternal presence
And with all God's people
And with heaven itself
To sing your praise.

Eucharistic Preface 5

Enriching, enlivening God,
It is indeed right
To give you thanks and praise.
You birthed your people
In labour and in joy
And fed us from the
Breast of Christ,
Who passed
Through blood and water
To bring us to the knowledge and love
Of your eternal presence.
And so we lift our hearts
With all the saints
To give you praise.

BLESSINGS AND ENDINGS

A closing blessing may contain either or both of two sections: first, praying that God be with us as we go out and do God's work in the world; and second, concluding with a Trinitarian blessing, making explicit that we are calling on the Christian, Trinitarian God.

This presents the opportunity to try out an alternative Trinitarian formulation from the standard Father, Son and Holy Spirit.

Creator, Redeemer and Sustainer/Inspirer is a popular option, although open to the charge that it is modalist; that is, representing three modes of being rather than three distinct persons. This presents a challenge to all redefinitions, and one may have to consider which is the least harmful option, and how important this (male-defined) heresy is. After all, if all our God-language is provisional, and pointing towards, rather than capturing, no words will be perfect.

However, one could instead seek to use a personal Trinitarian formula such as Sallie McFague's (1989) 'Mother, Lover, Friend', or Elizabeth Johnson's 'Spirit Sophia, Mother Sophia, Jesus Sophia' (2002, pp. 13–14, 131–97, 245–9). *Common Worship* offers, 'Source, Eternal Word and Holy Spirit' (2005, p. 648), and David Cunningham, 'Source, Wellspring and Living Water' (Read 2024, p.10). Or, substitute your own, prayerful understanding of the Trinity.

You can also make it responsive, as in the second example below.

Blessing 1

The rich blessing
Of the God
Who calls us into darkness
Be upon each one of us,
In our searching, in our stumbling,
In our longing,
And bring us ever closer
Into you.
Amen.

Blessing 2, Advent

May the God who calls to us from the depths
Open our ears.
Amen.

May the God who comes to us enwombed with longing
Melt our hearts.
Amen.

And may the God who encourages us
Send us out with joy.
Amen.

And the blessing of God, Creator, Redeemer and Sustainer be upon each one of us and all those whom we love, this day, this Advent and evermore.
Amen.

6

Examples and Resources: Services

A STRUCTURE FOR MORNING PRAYER

O God, open our lips,
And our mouth shall proclaim your praise.

Prayer of thanksgiving

Blessed are you, God beyond,
You create, redeem and sustain us.
You were in the beginning
And you are fresh every day.
Your holy vision guides us
And your eternal love holds us.
We thank you for all that you are
And for all that you have created us to be.
We pray that we may approach you
In confidence and faith,
Knowing you are our God
And we are your people.
Blessed be God forever.

The night has passed and the day lies open before us,
Let us pray with one heart and mind.

Silence

Holy God, we rejoice in this new day,
A continuance of all that is
And yet a new beginning.
Help us to live out your holy vision
Afresh, with hope, with daring
And surrounded by your love.
Amen.

The Word of God

Psalm: from *The Saint Helena Psalter*

Glory to God,
Source of all being,
Eternal Word
And Holy Spirit
Amen.

Reading 1

Canticle

Reading 2

Gospel Canticle

Intercessions

God among us,
Mercifully hear us.

Collect

Alternative Lord's Prayer 2019 (see pp. 49–50)

Ending

May the eternal God bless us,
Protect us and inspire us
This day and always.
Amen.

Let us bless the Holy Name,
Thanks be to God.

SERVICE OF THE WORD

The next few examples are of a non-Eucharistic service. In the Anglican context, this is called a Service of the Word (SOTW). The Appendix contains more information on the essential elements of this service, so I suggest comparing it with short services in your own tradition and adapting it accordingly.

The first SOTW is from a clergy conference workshop I led for Peterborough Diocese in 2023, where the audience was people who were longing for inclusive liturgy, together with those who were uncertain, apprehensive. The theme of the conference was 'Rejoice in Hope'. My aim was to make this gender inclusive, but very much on theme, and also, to avoid alienating those for whom this was new and strange, by retaining much that was familiar.

People from both categories reacted positively. Some of those who were already supportive and keen found it liberating and deeply moving, the image of being pregnant with the holy spirit experienced as particularly powerful, and some of those who were apprehensive were relieved that it was recognizably Anglican and still facilitated worship.

SERVICE OF THE WORD
Peterborough Diocese 2023: Rejoice in Hope

May the grace, hope and joy
Of the Holy Spirit
Be with you all.
And also with you.

For all that has been,
Thanks.

To all that shall be,
Yes.[1]

Collect: Janet Morley, 'Visitation of Mary to Elizabeth'[2]

Reading

Isaiah 52.7–10[3]
Romans 15.13
Mark 1.14b

Song: 'Sizohamba Naya' (We Will Go Rejoicing)[4]

Reflection

Prayers

God of hope,
You sent your prophets to change our hearts,
To bring us the hope of new life,
And in the word made flesh that new life came among us.

Help us always to hope in you,
To trust in your word,
And to be your agents in this world
For liberation from all that darkens.

---

1 Hammarskjöld, 1964, p. 87.
2 Janet Morley, 1992, p. 27.
3 NRSV, adapted, using 'I AM' for 'the Lord' and 'she' instead of 'he'.
4 Swaziland traditional hymn, tr., Wild Goose Resource Group, 2002.

God of hope,
Empower us.

God of joy,
Mary and Elizabeth rejoiced
In the new life you wrought within them,
And in the holding and the birthing and the nurturing
 of that new life.
Help us to open ourselves to your quickening,
To welcome and to nurture all that comes from you,
To set aside fear and complacency
And to bring your joy to the world.

God of joy,
Open us to new life.

God of love,
Your servant Paul taught us 'faith, hope, and love remain …
 and the greatest of these is love' (1 Cor. 13.13).
Help us to dwell in your love,
To ground all that we are and all that we do
In love for you, for each other, for ourselves.

God of love,
Fill us.

Alternative Lord's Prayer 2019 (see pp. 49–50)

Blessing

May the God of all our hope
Dwell within us,
May the God of all our joy
Burst forth among us,
And may the God of all love
Birth us into new life.
And the blessing of the triune God,
Creator, Redeemer and Sustainer,
Be upon us and remain with us
This day, this week and evermore.
Amen.

SERVICE OF THE WORD IN LENT
Wilderness

Gathering

As we journey with empty hands
And uncertain steps,
Open our eyes, O God,
To your luminous darkness.
That our heart may proclaim your praise.

Confession

We have faltered and lost faith.
God, have mercy.

We have stumbled in the darkness and cried out against you.
Christ, have mercy.

We have judged ourselves to have arrived
But not with you.
God, have mercy.

Give us the sorrow that heals
And the joy that praises[1]
That we may know ourselves forgiven, loved and free.
Amen.

Collect

Ever-living, ever-loving God,
The I AM to whom we turn in the darkness,
Give us courage as we enter the desert,
Feed us with truth in our wilderness
And enable us to rise to the full height
Of our blossoming,
As the rains come, the parched land renews
And we are restored.

---

1 David Stancliffe and Br Tristam SSF, 1994, p. 167.

We ask this in the name of the one in three
The three in one,
Source, Saviour, Sustainer.
Amen.

Liturgy of the Word

Genesis 16.1–2, 4, 6b–10, 13
Genesis 21.9–10, 14–16, 17b–20

Reflection

Prayers

God of the desert,
You come to us
When all is lost
And show us your reality.

Help us to dwell in that reality,
To welcome it,
To carry it with us
In whatever is to come.

In your fierce mercy,
Hear our prayer.

God of the outcast,
The despised,
The rejected,
The lost,

Come to us
In our lostness,
In our despair
And give us life.

In your fierce mercy,
Hear our prayer.

God of the haughty,
Of those who seek,
Their own solutions
And then break upon them,

Forgive us our lack of faith,
Our search for control,
Our failure to be kind.
May we know our need of you.

In your fierce mercy,
Hear our prayer.

Silent prayer

In your fierce mercy,
Hear our prayer.

Song: The Como Mamas: 'Out of the Wilderness'[2]

Alternative Lord's Prayer 2019 (see pp. 49–50)

Blessing

May the irrepressible mercy of
The God of Hagar and of Sarah
Pour out upon you,
Richly bless your wandering,
Your searching
And your suffering,
And may you emerge
Into the life to which God has called you,
Strong and tall and free.
Amen.

---

2 At https://www.youtube.com/watch?v=MDUjLGU-jXM (accessed 04.04.2025).

SERVICE OF THE WORD
Scottish Episcopal Church

This service was written for a Liturgy Writing Workshop in 2021 that I prepared for a group of people in the Scottish Episcopal Church. The group were preparing inclusive worship for a conference to be held in April 2021, 'Responding to the Sacred: Gender and Liturgy in Conversation', which was in alignment with a national review of their liturgy. The worship was intended to kickstart the discussion, using material designed to stimulate the imagination.

Greeting

May the God of restless justice
Inflame and inspire you.
**May she be with us
Between us and among us.**

Confession

Let us confess our sins
To the God who longs for our fulfilment.

Silence

God who breathed on the formless void,
And brought it to life,
You have made us in your image.
Forgive us our failure to
Believe, inhabit and accept our glory,
And our readiness to bow down to false images.

God, have mercy.
God, have mercy.

God of rushing wind,
You tear through our complacent landscapes
Changing everything.
Forgive us for the times when we
Cling to the familiar,

Fear to embrace the new
And step back from the challenge of the real.

Christ, have mercy.
Christ, have mercy.

God of fire and flame,
You have burned with desire
To melt the cold fear that holds us back,
To consume our hesitancy and self-doubt,
To send us out burning with your eternal message,
And we have turned away,
Polished our chains, nurtured our fears
And failed to risk liberation.

God, have mercy.
God, have mercy.

Absolution

May the God of wind and flame
Tear through our falsity,
Burn up our hesitancy
And inflame us with love.
Amen.

Song: Iona: 'I will Sing a Song of Love'[1]

Collect

Eternal God,
You long to purify us
Of all that makes us lesser.
Breathe on us today
And bring us to the fullest of life,
Burn in us
And give us courage,

---

[1] Iona: 'I will Sing a Song of Love', on *I will sing not sing alone*, available at https://www.youtube.com/watch?v=ysGf6g772vk (accessed 04.04.2025).

Inspire and delight us
That we may sing your song of love.
In the name of that love we pray.
Amen.

Liturgy of the Word

Iona: 'Lord, to whom shall we go?'[2]
Includes John 6.68 (chorus); 14.6, 15.5, 15.16, 11.25

Reflection

Prayers

Creator God,
May your sweet breath
Whisper in us today,
Your gentle touch
Loosen all that binds,
And your loving presence
Infuse our hearts and minds.

God of life,
Fill us.

Redeemer God,
May your fierce challenge
Overturn our tables,
Your suffering passion
Inspire our compassion,
And your rising again
Lift us into new life.

God of life,
Fill us.

---

[2] Iona: 'Lord, to whom shall we go?', on *Come all you people*, available at https://www.ionabooks.com/product/lord-to-whom-shall-we-go-reading-downloadable-music-track/ (accessed 04.04.2025).

Spirit God,
May we be woven into the community of your love,
May we share the playfulness
Of your dance,
And may we be sustained and inspired
By your persistent presence.

God of life,
Fill us.

Alternative Lord's Prayer

God of all creation,
In your presence we rejoice.
May your liberating song
Fill the earth,
Your harmony
Echo into eternity.
Fill us with all that we need
And forgive our faltering ways,
The ways in which we fail
Our neighbours and ourselves.
Give us forgiving hearts
For all that fails us,
And help us to resist the temptations
That keep us trapped.
For you have the words of eternal life,
You have the love that burns,
And the mercy that gentles.
You have, you are, all that we need
Now and forever.
Amen.

Blessing

May the God from whom we take our being
Give us life,
The God who came among us
Lead us out of suffering and into joy,
And may God our friend
Be with us on the way.

And the blessing of God
Creator, Redeemer and Sustainer,
Be upon us
This morning, this day
And evermore.
Amen.

SERVICE OF LAMENT AND HOPE
Synod Fringe Meeting: 10 July 2023

This service was offered by WATCH[1] as an opportunity to lament the historic and ongoing exclusion of women from ordination and from teaching and leading roles within the Church, an exclusion that has led to women's voices not being heard, their gifts and vocations not being recognized. As women, we stood with all those who have been excluded and marginalized due to sexuality, ethnicity, class, ability and disability and for whatever reason. We also chose to end on a note of hope.

Welcome and Introduction

The God of Rachel and of Judith and of Mary be with you,
And also with you.

Confession

We are the body of Christ, yet we have failed to honour all equally.
Merciful God,
Forgive us.

We are the body of Christ, yet we have crucified goodness and failed to heed the prophetic voice.
Merciful Christ,
Forgive us.

We are the body of Christ, but we have accepted the denigrations of others and failed to rise to our full height.
Merciful God,
Forgive us.

May God, who is merciful, compassionate and free, burn away our sin and inflame us with new and abundant life.
Amen.

---

[1] A subgroup from WATCH Executive Committee discussed and planned this service before I wrote the liturgy.

Collect

God of fire and flame,
In whose holy embrace we come to life,
Fill us we pray
With your cleansing fire,
Purify us with your holy desire
And strengthen us with your rightful rage.
We ask this in the name of the one
Who overturned the tables in the temple,
Who died and rose again, for love.
Amen.

Readings

Psalm 13.1–4
Lamentations 1.16
John 11.35 (KJV)

Song: John Bennet, The King's Singers, 'Weep, O mine eyes'[2]

Reflection

Litany of penitence for the denial of women's authority[3]

Revelation 22.1–2

The Lord's Prayer[4]

---

[2] John Bennet, The King's Singers, 'Weep O mine eyes', at https://www.youtube.com/watch?v=totNCMNNXQ8 (accessed 04.04.2025).
[3] Janet Morley, 1992, pp. 6–61, adapted for the context (accessed 04.04.2025).
[4] The Lord's Prayer, at https://livinghour.org/lords-prayer/new-zealand-maori/ (accessed 04.04.2025).

Act of commitment

We have named our pain
And laid it on the altar of the Most High.

We have cried our tears
And shed them with the one who wept for us.

We have brought our outrage
And placed it by the sword of your wrath.

And now we say, with the psalmist:
[Yet] I put my trust in your mercy,
My heart is joyful because of your saving help.
I will sing to the Holy One, who has dealt with me richly,
I will praise the Name of God Most High. (Psalm 13.5–6)

Anointing

We anoint each other, with the words,
Go forth blessed by the God who sees you.

Hymn

'To be a pilgrim' *(replacing 'he' and 'him' with 'she' and 'her')*

Blessing and Dismissal

May the God of Hagar
See you into life,
The God of Elizabeth
Make you fruitful,
And the God of Mary Magdalene
Send you forth as an apostle to the world,
And the blessing of God,
Creator, Redeemer and Inspirer,
Be with us all
This evening, this Synod and
All the days and nights that are to come
Until we are gathered into
The eternal arms
Of God herself.
Amen.

SERVICE OF THE WORD
The Annunciation

Grace, mercy and peace
Be with you all,
And also with you.

Reading

Nicola Slee, 'Beatitude'[1]

Collect

God of the impossible,
You draw near
And open our hearts
To daring.
Give us the boldness of Mary,
Her capacity to trust in
Your outrageous promise,
Her courage
To walk an untested path,
Her willingness
To carry your living Word.
We ask this in the name of
The one whom Mary birthed,
Our vulnerable Saviour
Jesus Christ.
Amen.

Reading

Luke 1.26–38 (Inclusive Bible)

---

[1] Nicola Slee, 'Blessed is she ...', 2007, p. 22.

Song

Carol of the Annunciation, text by John Bell, Iona Community, 'No Wind at the Window'[2]

From 'Magnificat'[3]

Prayers

Let us pray.

Astounding God,
The God of Mary,
The God who suddenly comes near,
Swell our bellies with the shock of your presence
And lead us forward on the path
From which there is no turning back,
The path to life.

God of our foremothers,
Hear us.

Engendering Spirit,
You wait for our consent.
Give us the courage, like Mary,
To say YES,
Yes to the body's ripening,
Yes to the womb's shedding,
Yes to the life that comes
From our tender, glorious bodies
Into our vulnerable, glorious world.

God of our foremothers,
Hear us.

---

[2] Carol of the Annunciation, text by John Bell, Iona Community, 'No Wind at the Window', at https://www.youtube.com/watch?v=A4oRuvTSjWA (accessed 04.04.2025).
[3] Nicola Slee, 2007, pp. 61–2.

God of our whole lives,
May our Yes to you
Remain open,
Even when the visitation ends,
When your radiant presence
Is but memory,
And our ripeness and fullness
Are passing into decay.
Nourish our aging,
Sharpen our wisdom,
And accompany us as we move closer
To the eternity that awaits us.

God of our foremothers,
Hear us.

An Alternative Lord's Prayer 2019 (see pp. 49–50)

Blessing

May the God of sudden appearings
And startling offers,
The God who longs to be born in us,
Bless you,
Fill you with life
And send you forth rejoicing.
Amen.

SERVICE OF THE WORD FOR ADVENT

Yes, I am coming soon!
Amen, Come, Jesus!
(Revelation 22.20, Inclusive Bible)

In the quiet and the waiting,
Come, Jesus, come.
In the holding and the hoping,
Come, Jesus, come.

In the darkness and the longing,
Come, Jesus, come.

Confession

We have failed to embrace quiet,
To honour waiting,
Rushing on to our next task,
Turning time into our enemy.

God, have mercy.
God, have mercy.

Impatient for more
We have let go
What we should have held,
And squandered hope on illusion.

Christ, have mercy.
Christ, have mercy.

We have feared the darkness,
Longing for rescue,
Instead of growing
We have shrivelled.

God, have mercy.
God, have mercy.

May we know ourselves held
In the womb of God,
In the bright darkness of

God's eternal love,
Where all things are known
And we are made whole.
Amen.

Collect

God of Advent,
Enwombed by Mary,
Waiting to be born
In the darkness of the stable night.
Hold us
In your gracious arms
All the days and nights of our life.
Realize our hope
And love us into growth
That we may reflect
Your glorious humility
And your patient eternity.
Amen.

Song: John Tavener, 'Mother of God here I stand'[1]

Reading: Luke 1.26–38 (Inclusive Bible)

We believe …

We believe in the God who birthed us,
The God who visits us
And the God who sustains us.
Amen.

We believe in the God
Who seeks our growth,
Awaits our yes
And never leaves us.
Amen.

---

[1] John Tavener, 'Mother of God here I stand', at https://www.youtube.com/watch?v=UnS1mRAd57I&feature=youtu.be (accessed 04.04.2025).

We believe in the everlasting,
The everyday,
And the time to come.
Amen.

We commit ...

Lancelot Andrews, adapted[2]

Prayers: Jan Berry, 'God of Waiting'[3]

Alternative Lord's Prayer

God of time and space,
Who comes to us here on earth
In your fullness we rejoice.
May your eternal goodness reign
In all places and all times
So that we may grow.
Enable us to reject the temptation of falsity
And the evil of lies,
To overcome it with your immense truth
Until the world is filled with the forgiveness
Of the absolute
And all distortions gone.
For you alone give us the power
The hope and the glory
This day and forever.
Amen.

Blessing: Ruth Burgess, '4th Sunday of Advent, Cycle A Blessing'[4].

---

2 Lancelot Andrews, 2004, adapted, in David Adam, p. 38.
3 Jan Berry, 2009, pp. 156–7.
4 Ruth Burgess, 2005, p. 67.

SERVICE OF THE WORD WITH HOLY COMMUNION: LIBERATION

I offered this to the women clergy of St Alban's Diocese in September 2023, after delivering a talk on Gender Inclusive Liturgy. I used Eucharistic Prayer G from Common Worship: Services and Prayers, *with some adaptations to replace instances of 'he', 'Lord' and 'Father'. The theme for the service was Liberation.*

Greeting

May the God of liberating joy
Be with you.
And also with you.

Confession

God of freedom,
We bring to you all those ways in which we have enchained ourselves and others.

We have failed to dare the narrow path
of justice and mercy,
To walk humbly with you our God,
Seeking instead the approval of others
and our own convenience.

Kyrie, eleison.
Kyrie, eleison.

We have closed our eyes to suffering
And our ears to the cries of the oppressed,
We have failed to set the prisoners free.

Christe, eleison.
Christe, eleison.

We have allowed others to limit our power
And neglected to stand up and flourish.

Kyrie, eleison.
Kyrie, eleison.

May the God of love
Who calls us to richness and depth,
Free us from the smallness that beckons
And liberate us into fullness of life.
In the name of Jesus, born of Mary.
Amen.

Collect

O God our deliverer,
Who sent Jesus, born of a woman
To live among us,
Proclaiming liberation to the captives and
Honouring the dishonoured,
Lift us up
That we may enter into your reign of glory
Cherished, strong and free.
Through Christ our liberator.
Amen.

The Word

Exodus 6.6–9 (NRSVUE, adapted so 'LORD' is replaced on the first occasion by 'God' and subsequently by 'the One'; alternatively, use *The Inclusive Bible*)

Reflection

Song: The Coma Mamas, 'Out of the Wilderness'[1]

Reading: John 8.32 (NRSV)

---

[1] The Coma Mamas, 'Out of the Wilderness, 2014, Daptone Records, https://www.youtube.com/watch?v=XU9N2v1fcKM (accessed 04.04.2025).

Discussion

Turn to your neighbour and talk for two minutes about your responses to these readings. Perhaps you'll want to talk about hope, or the truth that will set you free, or share your pondering on wilderness, or liberation, or something else ...

Prayers

God of fire,
You burn up the dross of our lives.
May your refining flames
Destroy all that imprisons and reduces us
And may we burn with your holy love.

God, in your mercy,
Hear our prayer.

Tender God,
You seek to gentle the wounded
To heal and to nourish
And to carry us into new life.
Help us express that love to those around us who need it.

God, in your mercy,
Hear our prayer.

Faithful God,
You accompany us through all our journeying,
Our despair, our hope and our liberation.
Help us to trust in you
And hold our hope for us when we have none.

God, in your mercy,
Hear our prayer.

Merciful God,
Accept these prayers
For the sake of
Our Saviour Jesus Christ
Amen.

The Liturgy of the Sacrament

God of peace, you come to us in all the moments of our lives,
if we but open our hearts to you.

The peace of God be with you all.
And also with you.

The God who liberates is here.
Her Spirit is with us.

Lift up your hearts.
We lift them to our God.

Let us give thanks to the God of grace.
It is right to give thanks and praise.

Blessed are you, Liberating God,
Our light and our salvation,
To you be glory and praise for ever.
From the beginning you have created all things
And all your works echo the silent music of your praise.
In the fullness of time you made us in your image,
The crown of all creation.
You give us breath and speech, that with angels and archangels
And all the powers of heaven
We may find a voice to sing your praise.

Holy, holy, holy One,
God of power and might,
Heaven and earth are full of your glory.
Hosanna in the highest.
Blessed is the one who comes in the name of the Lord.
Hosanna in the highest.

How wonderful the work of your hands, O God.
As a mother tenderly gathers her children
You embraced a people as your own.
When they turned away and rebelled
Your love remained steadfast.
From them you raised up Jesus our Saviour, born of Mary,
To be the living bread
In whom all our hungers are satisfied.

He offered his life for sinners,
And with a love stronger than death
He opened wide his arms on the cross.
On the night before he died
He came to supper with his friends,
And, taking bread, he gave you thanks.
He broke it and gave it to them, saying,
'Take, eat; this is my body which is given for you
Do this in remembrance of me.'
At the end of supper, taking the cup of wine
He gave you thanks, and said,
'Drink this, all of you; this is my blood of the new covenant
Which is shed for you and for many for the forgiveness of sins.
Do this, as often as you drink it, in remembrance of me.'

Great is the mystery of faith.
Christ has died.
Christ is risen.
Christ will come again.

God our Source and our Sustainer, we plead with confidence
His sacrifice made once for all upon the cross.
We remember his dying and rising in glory
And we rejoice that he intercedes for us at your right hand.
Pour out your Holy Spirit as we bring before you
These gifts of your creation,
May they be for us the body and blood of your dear Son.
As we eat and drink these holy things in your presence,
Form us in the likeness of Christ
And build us into a living temple to your glory.
Bring us at the last with all the saints
To the vision of that eternal splendour
For which you have created us.
Through Jesus Christ
By whom, with whom, and in whom,
With all who stand before you in earth and heaven
We worship you, God almighty, in songs of everlasting praise.
Blessing and honour and glory and power
Be yours for ever and ever.
Amen.

Alternative Lord's Prayer[2]

Breaking of the Bread

We break this bread
To share in the body of Christ.
Though we are many, we are one body
Because we all share in one bread.

Jesus, Lamb of God,
Have mercy on us.
Jesus, bearer of our sins,
have mercy on us.
Jesus, redeemer of the world,
Grant us peace.

Giving of Communion

God's holy gifts
For God's holy people.
Jesus Christ is holy.
Jesus Christ reigns
To the glory of Almighty God.

Almighty God,
We thank you for feeding us
With the body and blood of your Son Jesus Christ.
Through him we offer you our souls and bodies
To be a living sacrifice.
Send us out
In the power of your Spirit
To live and work
To your praise and glory.
Amen.

---

[2] At https://worshipwords.co.uk/our-father-our-mother-parallel-versions-orchard-ridge-wisconsin-usa/ (accessed 04.04.2025).

Post Communion

Keep, Holy God, your Church, with your perpetual mercy,
And, because without you our human frailty cannot but fall,
Keep us ever by your help from all things hurtful
And lead us to all things profitable to our salvation,
Through Jesus Christ our Saviour.[3]
Amen.

Blessing

May the God of all our longings,
Who comes in love to break our chains,
Stir us with her Holy Spirit
And open our hearts
To her eternal freedom.
And may the blessing of God
Creator, Redeemer and Sustainer
Be upon us
And all those whom we love
This day and evermore.
Amen.

Go in the peace of Christ.
Thanks be to God.

---

[3] *Common Worship: Services and Prayers*, 2000, Post Communion prayer for Ordinary time after Pentecost.

A LITURGY OF BECOMING

*Written for a WATCH Committee Meeting in July 2024.
This was deliberately crafted to be inclusive of
all gender identities.*

Greeting

The grace of the Most High God be with you.
And also with you.

Gloria

Glory to you, God beyond us.
You call us to lift our eyes
To your uncreated glory,
To unimagined realms of heaven.

Glory to you, God among us.
You spoke and your Word had substance,
It took on flesh
Our flesh.
You lived, you grew,
You suffered and died among us,
You showed us incarnate love.

Glory to you, God between us.
You breathed and your Spirit came,
The Spirit who hovered on the chaos,
Who is with us now,
Who excites and beckons us to realize
All that can be, all that will be,
All that for which we were created.

Glory to you, God of all.
You call us into being.

Confession

We come before you as your children, your co-creators, your joy, but in recognition that we are not yet all that we could be; we do not yet fully embrace the becoming that exists in your glorious vision.

And so we pray.

Creator God,
Forgive our refusal to grow,
Our hesitation to change
The inertia that we cling to
For misguided comfort.

Maker of all,
Have mercy on us.

God of all people,
Forgive us those times
When we have rejected others,
Confined when we should have liberated,
Criticized when we should have enabled.

Maker of all,
Have mercy on us.

God of our inmost depths,
Forgive our self-limitation, our fear
And make us takers of new steps,
Risk-takers,
Life-livers,
Love-givers.

Maker of all,
Have mercy on us.

Absolution

God of grace, mercy and life,
We claim your forgiveness
For our weakness and our fear,
And we embrace your liberating power
To become a new creation.
Amen.

Collect

God of new beginnings,
Who, like a proud parent
Delights in our arrival
And rejoices in our growth,
Help us to weave lives of authenticity
Threaded with justice and truth,
That we may reflect your glory
In our fractured world.
In the name of the one who
Walked an authentic path
Fearless and vulnerable
Our Saviour Jesus Christ.
Amen.

Readings

Genesis 1.1–2 (NRSV)
1 Corinthians 13.9–13 (NRSV)

Song: Salt of the Sound, 'Peace, With You'[1]

Reading: John 16.12–14 (Inclusive Bible)

---

1 Salt of the Sound, 'Peace, With You', 2014, at https://www.youtube.com/watch?v=9WtodyYztqM (accessed 04.04.2025).

Creed[2]

I believe in God,
Life giver, life liver, life enabler.
I believe in God,
Who created us,
Who came among us and
Who rejoices with us as we live and grow.

I believe in God,
Uncreated, yet born of a woman,
Eternal, yet in time,
Crucified and yet triumphant.
This is our faith.
Alleluia,
Amen.

Prayers

Music: Anita Tatlow and Salt of the Sound, 'Vespers'[3]

Provide butterfly shapes for people to write prayers on.
On one side, write or draw something you wish to leave behind, that does not represent your truest self. Pray with this.
Then turn the butterfly over.
On the other side, write or draw something new and life-giving that you feel called to, or ask for inspiration to discern how you might grow in truth and beauty. Pray with this.
Place the butterfly in the basket on the altar when you are finished.

Let us pray.

Eternal God, Father, Mother, Parent of us all,
We pray that you will be with us as we journey,

---

[2] Anglicans are required to use a profession of faith as stipulated in *Common Worship: Daily Prayer*, 2005.
[3] Anita Tatlow and Salt of the Sound, 'Vespers', 2024, at https://www.youtube.com/watch?v=9yj_DIotJdM (accessed 04.04.2025).

That you will show us new vistas and
Unexpected ways of being.
Resource us to make choices that
Liberate our true selves.

God of mercy,
Hear us.

God our friend,
Help us to find companions along the way,
Who encourage and empower us,
Who lead us into truth.
Help us to be that friend to others,
Open our ears to the cries of the lonely and confused,
And open our hearts to care as you do
For the liberation of all.

God of mercy,
Hear us.

God our inspiration,
Hover over our chaos
And break open
The mind-forged manacles of our own fear.
Breathe new thoughts in us
And connect us with each other and with you
That all that is life-giving and fresh may emerge
With your holy blessing.

God of mercy,
Hear us.

Alternative Lord's Prayer

Mother,
God beyond,
Father,
God beyond,
Loving parent,
God beyond,
Touch us with your glory and open the voice of our praise.

May all that you envisage for us
Come to pass
That our lives may be touched by your eternal mercy
And transformed by love.
Feed us with all that we need to grow
And forgive us when we resist that growth
As we forgive those who put
Obstacles in our path.
Help us to resist the temptation to stay safe,
But keep us from reckless danger,
For you are the imprint of all that is
Creative, alive and free
Now and eternally.
Amen.

Blessing

We conclude our liturgy by praying to the God who is three in one and one in three,
That they may visit us with their gracious favour.

May God our source
Accompany us as we journey in self-discovery,
May God who lived among us
Show herself in our daily lives,
And may the Spirit outpoured
Inspire us with their gentle wisdom.

May the Holy Three,
In whom are contained all people and all things,
Be with us and may they remain with us
As we journey on.
Amen.

SERVICE OF THE WORD
Hope

May God, who in her wisdom
Came among us as a little baby,
Be with you all.
And also with you.

The Venite

1 O come, let us sing to God,
   let us heartily rejoice in the rock of our salvation.
2 **Let us come into her presence with thanksgiving
   and be glad in her with psalms.**
3 For God is a great God,
   great above all gods.
4 **In her hand are the depths of the earth
   and the heights of the mountains are hers also.**
5 The sea is hers, for she made it,
   and her hands have moulded the dry land.
6 **Come, let us worship and bow down
   and kneel before God our Maker.**
7 For she is our God,
   we are the people of her pasture and the sheep of her hand.
   Glory be to God, Source of all being, Eternal Word and
   Holy Spirit.

Collect

O Holy Wisdom,
Breath of God,
Word of God,
Presence of God,
Love of God,
Come among us with your fierce glory,
Illuminate our darkness
And set us free to hope.
We make this prayer to you,
Present in all things from the beginning of time,

Present with us now
In hope and joy.
Amen.

Reading: Wisdom 7.22–8.1

Song: 'O Wisdom, breathed from God (O Sapientia)'[1]

Reading: Malcolm Guite, 'O Sapientia An Advent Antiphon'[2]

Song: Anita Tatlow, 'Grounded' and 'Salt of the Sound'[3]

Prayers

God of hope,
We bring before you those times
When we are hopeless,
When darkness surrounds us
And despair prevails.

We bring to you all those in our world
Currently in darkness,
The persecuted,
The hungry,
Those living with war, invasion and hatred,
The people of Ukraine, of Israel and Palestine[4]
And all other suffering places in our world.

Scatter the darkness
By the grace of your holy presence,
Fill us with the light of your love
And show us a path to life.

---

1 'O Wisdom, breathed from God (O Sapientia)', at https://www.youtube.com/watch?v=moMPbx5MUdw (accessed 04.04.2025).
2 Malcolm Guite, 'O Sapientia An Advent Antiphon', at https://malcolmguite.files.wordpress.com/2016/12/17-o-sapienta.jpg (accessed 04.04.2025).
3 Anita Tatlow, 'Grounded' and 'Salt of the Sound', at https://open.spotify.com/track/3pn7dyowHcmC6mrkQl2Vb9?si=87820ef7677f45c6 (accessed 04.04.2025).
4 Substitute current conflicts as required.

Service of the Word: Hope 93

God, in your mercy,
Hear our prayer.

God among us,
Help us to be life-livers
And hope-bringers.
Show us how to dare
To live your glorious freedom,
Break the shackles of our smallness
And liberate us
That we may be liberators of others.

God, in your mercy,
Hear our prayer.

Breath of God,
Breathe on us,
May we know your gentleness,
Your compassion and your peace
That we may breathe you in
And breathe you out
Into a world that longs for you
And where you long to be known.

God, in your mercy,
Hear our prayer.

Alternative Lord's Prayer 2019 (see pp. 49–50)

Blessing

May the breath of God inspire you,
The wisdom of God guide you
And the glory of God shine in you.
And the blessing of *the one/she* who is
Source, Word and Holy Spirit
Be upon you this day, this night and evermore.
Amen.

WATCH CONFERENCE 20 APRIL 2024
Finding Our Voices

Greeting

May the God of love and justice
Strengthen our hearts,
And give us voice.

Come among us,
Merciful God,
Take from us our fear,
Our slowness to speak,
Our diffidence.

Clothe us in the garments of salvation,
Equip us with the sword of justice,
Give us the words that we lack
And the inspiration we need,
That, filled with your Holy Spirit,
We may bring your grace and truth
To all we meet.

We ask this in the name of
The one who dared to question authority
And who remained clothed in your love.
Amen.

Hymn: Dan Schutte, 'I, the Lord of Sea and Sky', substituting 'God' for 'Lord'. Chorus: first time use 'Lord', second time 'Abba', third time 'Amma'.[1]

Reading: Mark 7.24–30, the Syrophoenician Woman (NRSV)

Reflection

Invite the people gathered, if they wish to do so, to write a prayer on post-its provided and put them on display boards around the room. Play music quietly.

---

[1] Dan Schutte, 1981, 'I, the Lord of Sea and Sky', at https://www.youtube.com/watch?v=UA2fMeXEKLA (accessed 04.04.2025).

Music: James MacMillan, 'O Radiant Dawn', Apollo 5[2]

Prayers

God of rushing wind,
Breathe in us,
Use these our words,
Our hopes and our longings
To bring healing and wholeness
To your broken world.

God of life and love,
Hear our prayer.

God of roaring water,
Drowning the oppressor in the Red Sea,
Encourage us
That we may be as the Syro-Phoenician woman,
Speaking out,
Daring to hope
That you may listen.

God of life and love,
Hear our prayer.

God who came to earth,
Show us how to be alongside
All those trapped in oppression.
Give us the strength of vulnerability
And the shining power of those who wield truth
That we may dare to be your newness in the world.

God of life and love,
Hear our prayer.

Alternative Lord's Prayer 2019 (see pp. 49–50)

Blessing: Janet Morley, 'Easter Blessing'[3]

---

[2] James MacMillan, 2019, 'Apollo 5: O Radiant Dawn', at https://www.youtube.com/watch?v=5drCQq73ZBE (accessed 04.04.2025).
[3] Janet Morley, 1992, p. 88.

A LITURGY OF TRANSITION

This liturgy is designed to support a person making a gender identity transition, including embracing a trans, non-binary and other gender queer identity.

Greeting

Come, glory of God who made us.
Shine upon us.

Come, tenderness of God who saves us.
Embrace us.

Come, playful Spirit who sustains us.
Dance among us.

Come, living God,
Be with us all.

Confession

Holy God,
You birth us with the potential to be full of life,
But we allow fear to thwart our flourishing.

God, have mercy.
God, have mercy.

You beckon us into something new,
But we limit our growth to what is known.

Christ, have mercy.
Christ, have mercy.

You call us to joyfully liberate the captives,
But we encourage submission to the norm.

God, have mercy.
God, have mercy.

Absolution

May the mercy of God
Drop down upon you like dew
And may you know yourself, forgiven,
Loved and free.
Amen.

Gloria

O come let us sing to God
Who made us as we are
And called us to what we can be.
Praise be to the God of the heights.

O come let us sing to God
Who saves us in the abyss,
The illusion of separation
From ourselves, each other, and from God.
Praise be to the God of the depths.

O come let us sing to God
Who remains among us
Wherever we are,
Who weaves together the heights and the depths.
Praise be to the God who contains all things.
Blessed be God forever.

Collect

Holy God,
You beckon us ever closer into you,
Calling us to leave behind
All that traps, all that is false,
All that entombs our flourishing.
Breathe on us today,
Encourage us into fearlessness
And equip us to serve you
In newness and in truth.
We ask this in the name of the one

Whose actions and words were as one,
Who showed us how to live authentically
Our Saviour Jesus Christ.
Amen.

Readings

Psalm 139.1–16, *Saint Helena Psalter*[1]
Or Carla A. Grosch-Miller, *Psalms Redux*[2]
Isaiah 43.1–2, 4a, 14–21
Gospel options: Luke 4.18–19; Mark 1.9–11; John 15.1–11; John 3.1–8; John 7.37–38

Affirmation of Baptismal Faith

Have you been baptized in the name of God, Creator, Redeemer and Inspirer?
I have.

Are you ready to affirm your baptismal vows?
I am.

What name do you take to go forward in the life of Christ?
Or
How will you be referred to?
What pronouns do you identify with to go forward in the life of Christ?
Use a sentence that is meaningful to you.[3]
Name is spoken / pronouns are given.

People of God, will you support and uphold N in *their*[4] life in Christ?
With the help of God we will.

---

[1] Order of St Helena, 2024.
[2] Carla A. Grosch-Miller, 2014.
[3] Some other way of affirming a trans or a nonbinary identity may be substituted here. This should be discussed with the person in advance of the service.
[4] Substitute another pronoun as required.

A Liturgy of Transition

The Decision

Do you reject the ways of darkness, and the paths of untruth?
I reject them.

Do you renounce all that binds and oppresses, those beliefs and actions that lead to the captivity of the soul?
I renounce them.

Do you repent of the deeds that separate us from God and neighbour?
I repent of them.

May God, who has called you as you are
To this moment and this place
Empower you to continue on the Way.
Amen.

Profession of Faith

I believe in God,
Life-maker,
Life-giver,
Life-sustainer.
I believe in God.

I believe in the Holy One,
In goodness,
Forgiveness
And love.
I believe in God

I believe in first gifts,
In second chances
And in holy renewal.
I believe in God.

I believe in God,
Source, Word and Holy Spirit.
I believe in God.
Amen.

Commission

Those who are baptized are called to worship and serve God.

Will you go forward as a person of faith, prayer and love?
With the help of God, I will.

Will you persevere when things are difficult,
Repent when you get things wrong,
Forgive yourself and others?
With the help of God, I will.

Will you seek to love others,
To reach out to those who are different,
To show generosity?
With the help of God, I will.

May Christ dwell within you,
May you be rooted and grounded in love,
And bring forth the fruit of the Spirit.
Amen.

Prayers

Those present have been asked to prepare a prayer they would like to say for the candidate/s.
All gather in a circle. This can either be around the altar or more informally, around a central, lit candle on a table.
Each lights a tealight and places it on the altar/table, then says their prayer.
The prayers are gathered up and concluded with an Alternative Lord's Prayer.

Alternative Lord's Prayer

Source of all,
Whose heavenly love
Births, re-births and sustains us,
We give you thanks
For all that is,
All that has been,
And all that will be.

We pray that your ways may break in on us
And that we may be bold to follow them,
That we may see heaven here on earth.
Give us food for the journey
And forgive us when we step away from your path.
Help us to follow you in forgiving others
Even as they reject us
And cause us pain.
Do not bring us to a trial that is too great for us
And save us from the death of the spirit.
For you are the power of love,
You are all that we need
Now and forever.
Amen.

Blessing

May you know the delight of God who made you,
The compassion of God who walks with you,
And the love of God who lives within you.
And the blessing of God,
Source, Word and Holy Spirit,
Be upon you this day, this night and evermore.
Amen.

Giving of a lighted candle

A lighted candle is given to the candidate

God has brought you out of darkness and into God's/*their* most marvellous light.

You have received the light of Christ,
Walk in this light all the days of your life.
Shine as a light in the world
To the glory of the God who loves you.

Dismissal

Go in the light and peace of Christ.
Thanks be to God.

7

Conclusion

Christians worship a God who is beyond gender, yet our liturgy continues to enshrine a male God while employing doublethink to maintain that this God isn't really male, even though the pronouns and images we use for 'him' are.

This is damaging to women, to men and to our mission. It is contrary to justice and pastoral care. It is not good for our relating to God, as we are using images that have ossified, that no longer provoke a lively connection with the divine.

We have an opportunity not just to revise our language for God by removing references to the 'male', but to diversify our images to enliven our connection with God by adding those that relate to female life and experience, and those that recognize the complexity of gender as we currently understand and live it.

In this book, I have explored the reasons why inclusive liturgy matters and defined my terms. I have provided some principles to take on board, with practical advice about how to proceed and bring people with you. I have given suggestions on how to write specific parts of the liturgy, as well as examples of what this liturgy might look like. I have also provided some resources to read and find inspiration. In the Appendix, I also cover the legal freedoms and opportunities that exist for Anglicans within Canon Law to write new, inclusive forms of liturgy, and to encourage the doubtful to grasp these.

Now it is down to you. Have a go! See what happens. You might be surprised at the enlivening that occurs, the new conversations about faith and God that are stimulated, the relief and gratitude that you encounter. And you might find you tread a new and lively path to God, for whom no words or images are big enough.

8

References and Resources

I include here the books mentioned in the text and a range of resources I have found useful, and hope you will too.

Scripture and tradition

Biblical

The Inclusive Bible: The First Egalitarian Translation © 2009, Rowman and Littlefield Publishers Inc.The King James Bible © the Crown and the Crown's Patentee, Cambridge University Press.

The New Revised Standard Version Bible: Anglicized Edition, © 1989, 1995, National Council of the Churches of Christ in the United States of America.

Matthew 23.37; Luke 13.34; Psalm 131.2; Isaiah 42.13–14; 66.11–13; Hosea 11.1–4; 1 Corinthians 3.2; 1 Thessalonians 2.7.

Other

Aelred of Rievaulx, *De institutione inclusarum*, Chs 26 and 31, 1, pp. 668–71, in M. P. Mcpherson, trans., 1971, *The Works of Aelred of Rievaulx*, 1: *Treatises and Pastoral Prayer*, Cistercian Fathers Series, Vol. 2, Spencer, MA: Liturgical Press, p. 73.

Anselm, *Opera omnia*, in F. S. Schmitt, ed., 1968, Stuttgart: Frommann, 3:33 and pp. 39–41.

Barton, John, 2022, *The Word: On the Translation of the Bible*, London: Penguin Books Ltd, especially Chapter 6.

Bell, John L. and Graham Maule, 2018, *Known Unknowns: 100 Contemporary Texts to Comon Tunes*, Glasgow: Wild Goose Publications.

Boyce-Tillman, June, 2003, *A Rainbow to Heaven: Hymns, Songs and Chants*, London: Stainer & Bell.

Bynum, Caroline Walker, 1989, 'Religious Women in the Later Middle Ages', in Jill Raitt, ed., *Christian Spirituality: High Middle Ages and Reformation*, London: SCM Press, pp. 121–39.

De Jesu puero duodenni, sect. 3, par. 31, in A. Hoste, C. H. Talbot and R. Vander Plaetse, eds, 1971, *Aelred, Opera omnia*, I, Corpus Christianorum Corpus Mediaevalis Series 1, Turnout, Belgium: Brepolis, pp. 277–8.

Durka, Gloria, 1989, *Praying with Julian of Norwich*, Winona, MN: St Mary's Press.

Order of St Helena, 2024, *The Saint Helena Psalter*, New York: Church Publishing Inc.
Wilmart, A., 1923, 'Introduction', in D. A. Castel, trans., *Méditations and prières de saint Anselme*, Collection Pax 11, Paris: P. Lethielleux/Desclee de Brouwer/Abbaye de Maredsous, pp. i–lxii, 48–61.
Windeatt, Barry, trans., 2015, Julian of Norwich, *Revelations of Divine Love*, Oxford: Oxford University Press.

Iona

The Iona Community, 2001, *Iona Abbey worship book*, Glasgow: Wild Goose Publications.
Neil Paynter, 2002, *This Is the Day: Readings and Meditations from the Iona Community*, Glasgow: Wild Goose Publications.

References and further reading

Adams, Graham, 2024, *God the Child: Small, Weak and Curious Subversions*, London: SCM Press.
Ahmed, Sara, 2021, 'Willfulness, Feminism, and the Gendering of Will', in Jude Browne, ed., *Why Gender?*, Cambridge: Cambridge University Press, pp. 245–66.
Allen RSM, Sr Prudence, 1997, *The Concept of Woman: The Aristotelian Revolution, 750 BC–AD 1250*, Grand Rapids, MI: W. B. Eerdmans.
Ambrose, Gill and Kershaw, Simon, 2001, *Come to the Feast*, Norwich: Canterbury Press, pp. 135–6.
Andrews, Lancelot, 2004, in Adam, David, ed., *Candles in the Dark*, Rattlesden: Kevin Mayhew.
The Anglican Church in Aotearoa, New Zealand and Polynesia, 1997, *A New Zealand Prayer Book*, New York: HarperOne.
Barton, John and John Muddiman, eds., 2014, *The Oxford Bible Commentary*, Oxford: Oxford University Press.
Berry, Jan, 2009, 'God of Waiting', in *Ritual Making Women: Shaping Rites for Changing Lives*, London: Routledge, pp. 156–7.
Brown, Rosalind, 2021, *Prayers for Living: 500 Prayers for Public and Private Worship*, Durham: Sacristy Press.
Browne, Jude, ed., 2021, *Why Gender?*, Cambridge: Cambridge University Press.
Bruce, Kate and Liz Shercliffe, 2024, *Preaching the Women of the Bible*, Vol. 2, London: SCM Press.
Burgess, Ruth, ed., 2005, *Candles and Conifers*, Glasgow: Wild Goose Publications.
Butler, Judith, 2021, 'Gender in Translation: Beyond Monolingualism', in Jude Browne, ed., *Why Gender?*, Cambridge: Cambridge University Press, pp.15–37.

Carden, John, ed., 1989, *With All God's People: The New Ecumenical Prayer Cycle*, Geneva: WCC Publications.
Chatti, Leila, 2020, *Deluge*, Washington: Copper Canyon Press.
Church of Scotland Panel on Worship, 1994, *Book of Common Order*, Edinburgh: St Andrew Press.
Common Worship: Daily Prayer, 2005, London: Church House Publishing.
Common Worship: Festivals, 2023, London: Church House Publishing.
Common Worship: Ordination Services, 2007, London: Church House Publishing.
Common Worship: Services and Prayers, 2000, London: Church House Publishing.
Common Worship: Times and Seasons, 2006, London: Church House Publishing.
Criado-Perez, Caroline, 2015, *Do it Like a Woman ... and Change the World*, London: Granta Publications.
Criado-Perez, Caroline, 2019, *Invisible Women: Exposing data bias in a world designed for men*, London: Chatto & Windus.
Daly, Mary, 1985, *Beyond God the Father: Towards a Philosophy of Women's Liberation*, London: The Women's Press.
de Beauvoir, Simone, 1973, *The Second Sex*, New York: Vintage Books.
Dupré, John, 2019, 'Gender and the End of Biological Determinism', in Jude Browne, ed., *Why Gender?*, Cambridge: Cambridge University Press, pp. 57–77.
Earey, Mark, 2011, *Finding Your Way Around Common Worship: A Simple Guide*, London: Church House Publishing.
Earey, Mark, 2013, *Beyond Common Worship: Anglican Identity and Liturgical Diversity*, London: SCM Press.
Earey, Mark and Phillip Tovey, 2009, *Liturgical Formation and Common Worship*, Cambridge: Grove Books Ltd.
Eiesland, Nancy L., 1994, *The Disabled God: Towards a Liberation Theology of Disability*, Nashville: Abingdon Press.
Faull, Vivienne and Jane Sinclair, 1986, *Count Us In: Inclusive Language in Liturgy*, Nottingham: Grove Books Ltd.
Foucault, Michel, 1980, 'Introduction', in Herculine Barbin, trans. Richard McDougall, *Herculine Barbin: Being the Recently Discovered Memoirs of a Nineteenth-Century French Hermaphrodite*, New York: Pantheon Books, pp. vii–xvii.
Gafney, Wilda, Year A, 2021, Year B, 2023, Year C, 2024, *A Women's Lectionary for the Whole Church: A Multi-Gospel Single Year Lectionary*, New York: Church Publishing Inc.
Geitz, Elizabeth Rankin, Marjorie A. Burke and Ann Smith, eds, 2000, *Women's Uncommon Prayers: Our Lives Revealed, Nurtured, Celebrated*, Harrisbury, PA: Morehouse Publishing.
Goldingay, John, 2010, *Genesis for everyone, Part I Chapters 1–16*, London: SPCK.
Grosch-Miller, Carla A., 2014, *Psalms Redux: Poems and Prayers*, Norwich: Canterbury Press.

Halberstam, Jack, 2021, 'Gender and the Queer/Trans Undercommons', in Jude Browne, ed., *Why Gender?*, pp. 38–56.

Hammarskjöld, Dag, 1964, *Markings*, London: Faber & Faber.

Hampson, Daphne, 1990, *Theology and Feminism*, Oxford: Blackwell Ltd.

Hampson, Michael (creator and publisher), 2025, *Sunday Scriptures for Reading Aloud*, The Complete 3 Year Lectionary (2025–28), https://ssra.uk, accessed 08.06.2025.

Isherwood, Lisa, 2007, *The Fat Jesus: Feminist Explorations in Boundaries and Transgressions*, London: Darton, Longman & Todd Ltd.

Jagger, Sharon, 2023, 'Presiding Like a Woman: Menstruating at the Altar', in Ashley Cocksworth, Rachel Starr and Stephen Burns, eds, *From the Shores of Silence*, London: SCM Press.

Johnson, Elizabeth, 2002, *She Who Is*, New York: The Crossroad Publishing Company.

Jones, Serene, 2000, *Feminist Theory and Christian Theology: Cartographies of Grace*, Minneapolis, MN: Fortress Press.

Keller, Catherine, 2003, *Face of the Deep: A Theology of Becoming*, Abingdon: Routledge.

King, Helen, 2013, *The One-Sex Body on Trial: The Classical and Early Modern Evidence*, Farnham, Ashgate.

King, Helen, 2024, *Immaculate Forms: Uncovering the History of Women's Bodies*, London: Profile Books Ltd.

Kleinman, Sherryl, 2002, 'Why sexist language matters', *Qualitative Sociology*, Vol. 25, No. 2, Summer, pp. 299–304.

Laqueur, Thomas, 1992, *Making Sex: Body and Gender from the Greeks to Freud*, Cambridge, MA and London: Harvard University Press.

Lawson Jacobs, N. and E. Richardson, 2022, *Disability, justice and the Churches*, London: Darton, Longman & Todd.

Lucas, Kayleigh, 2023, 'Why is exclusively male language, when talking about God, potentially damaging?', BA dissertation, Durham: Durham University Common Awards.

Mann, Rachel, 2015, *Star-filled Grace: Worship and Prayer Resources for Advent, Christmas & Epiphany*, Glasgow: Wild Goose Publications.

Manne, Kate, 2019, *Down Girl: The Logic of Misogyny*, London: Penguin Books.

McFague, Sallie, 1982, *Metaphorical Theology: Models of God in Religious Language*, Philadelphia, PA: Fortress Press.

McFague, Sallie, 1989, *Metaphorical Theology* and *Models of God: Theology for an Ecological, Nuclear Age*, Philadelphia, Fortress Press.

McFague, Sallie, 1996, 'Mother God', in Elizabeth Schüssler Fiorenza, ed., *The Power of Naming: A Concilium Reader in Feminist Liberation Theology*, London: SCM Press.

McGee, Lee, 1996, *Wrestling with the Patriarchs: Retrieving Women's Voices in Preaching*, Preacher's Library Series, Nashville, TN Abingdon Press.

Milton, G., 2022, *Celebrating Diversity in Christian Ritual: Honouring the Heritage of Minority Believers*, Cambridge: Grove Booklets Ltd.

Morley, Janet, ed., 1991, *Bread of Tomorrow*, London: SPCK.

Morley, Janet, ed., 1992, *All Desires Known*, London: SPCK.
O'Donnell, Karen, 2024, Introduction to Adams, Graham, *God the Child: Small, Weak and Curious Subversions*, London: SCM Press.
New Patterns for Worship, 2002, London: Church House Publishing.
Økland, Jorunn, 2004, *Women in Their Place*, LNTS, London: T & T Clark International.
Paveley, Rebecca, 2024, 'US bishops block move on baptism', *Church Times*, 24 May.
Paynter, Neil, 2002, *This is the day: Readings and meditations from the Iona Community*, Glasgow: Wild Goose Publishing.
Plater, Ormonde, 1995, *Intercession; A Theological and Practical Guide*, Boston, MA: Cowley Publications.
Powell, Lisa D., 2023, *The Disabled God Revisited: Trinity, Christology, and Liberation*, Edinburgh: T&T Clark.
Read, Charles, 2024, *Language, Gender, and God*, Cambridge: Grove Booklets Ltd.
Riley, Cole Arthur, 2024, *Black Liturgies: Prayers, Poems, and Meditations for Staying Human*, London: Hodder & Stoughton.
Roberts, Paul, 1999, *Alternative Worship in the Church of England*, Cambridge: Grove Booklets Ltd.
Rose, Margaret, Jenny Te Paa, Jeanne Person and Abigail Nelson, eds, 2009, *Lifting Women's Voices: Prayers to Change the World*, Norwich: Canterbury Press.
Sayer, Susan, 1997, 1999 and 2000, *Living Stones, The All-age Resource for Common Worship, Prayers of Intercession*, Lectionary Years A-C, Rattlesden: Kevin Mayhew Ltd.
Schüssler Fiorenza, Elisabeth, 1996, 'Breaking the Silence: becoming visible'; in Elisabeth Schüssler Fiorenza, ed., *The Power of Naming: A Concilium Reader in Feminist Liberation Theology*, London: SCM Press, pp.161–74.
Shakespeare, Steven, 2009. *Prayers for an Inclusive Church*, New York: Church Publishing.
Shercliff, Liz and Libby Lane, 2019, *Preaching Women: Gender, Power and the Pulpit*, London: SCM Press.
Slee, Nicola, 2022, *Abba Amma: Improvisations on the Lord's Prayer*, London: Canterbury Press, especially Chs 2–5.
Slee, Nicola, 2020, *Fragments for Fractured Times: What Feminist Practical Theology Brings to the Table*, London: SCM Press.
Slee, Nicola, 2024, *Praying Like a Woman*, London: SPCK.
Slee, Nicola, 2007, *The Book of Mary*, London: SPCK.
Slee, Nicola, 2011, *Seeking the Risen Christa*, London: SPCK.
Soskice, Janet, 2023, *Naming God: Addressing the Divine in Theology, Philosophy and Scripture*, Cambridge: Cambridge University Press.
Stancliffe, David and Br Tristam SSF, 1994, *Celebrating Common Prayer*, London, Mowbray.
Stevenson, Bishop Kenneth, 2004, *The Lord's Prayer: A Text in Tradition*, Minneapolis, Minnesota: Fortress Press.

Stuart, Elizabeth, 1992, *Daring to Speak Love's Name: A Gay and Lesbian Prayer Book*, London: Penguin Books.

Stuart, Elizabeth, 1995, *Just Good Friends: Towards a Lesbian and Gay Theology of Relationships*, London: Mowbray.

Tarrant, Ian, 2012, *Worship and Freedom in the Church of England: Exploring the Boundaries*, Cambridge: Grove Booklets Ltd.

Taylor, Charles, 2007, *A Secular Age*, Cambridge, MA: Harvard University Press.

Thatcher, Adrian, 2011, *God, Sex and Gender: An Introduction*, Chichester: Wiley-Blackwell.

Thatcher, Adrian, ed., 2017, *The Oxford Handbook of Theology, Sexuality and Gender*, Oxford: Oxford University Press.

Tillich, Paul, 1967, *Systematic Theology, 3 Volumes in 1*, Chicago: University of Chicago Press.

Vatican, Congregation for Catholic Education, June 10, 2019, *Male and Female He Created Them: Toward a Path of Dialogue on the Question of Gender Theory in Education*, Rome: Vatican City.

Von Rad, Gerhard, 1972, *Genesis*, London: SCM Press.

Walker, Alice, 2017, *The Color Purple*, London: Weidenfeld & Nicolson.

Ward, Hannah, Jennifer Wild, and Janet Morley, eds., 1995, *Celebrating Women*, London: SPCK.

Watson, Alice, 2019, *The (Re)Ritualisation of the Transition to Motherhood within the Church of England*, unpublished MA dissertation, University of Durham.

Watson, Natalie, 2003, *Feminist Theology*, Grand Rapids, MI: W. B. Eerdmans.

Wells, Sam and Abigail Kocher, 2016, *Joining the Angels' Song: Eucharistic Prayers for Sundays and Holy Days, Years A, B & C*, Norwich: Canterbury Press.

Wiles, Kate, 2003, *From Shore to Shore: Liturgies, Litanies and Prayers From Around the World*, London: SPCK, 2003.

Williams, N. and P. Brown, 2022, *Invisible Divides: Class, Culture and Barriers to Belonging in the Church*, London: SPCK.

Windeatt, Barry, trans., 2015, *Julian of Norwich: Revelations of Divine Love*, Oxford: Oxford University Press, pp. 128, 126, 131, 130, 131 for references to Christ our mother.

Winter, Miriam Therese, 1991, *WomanWisdom: A Feminist Lectionary and Psalter: Women of the Hebrew Scriptures*, Part 1, New York: Crossroad Publishing Company.

Media and online

The following websites were accessed on 8 July 2025

Adamson, Kelly, 2024, 'Women have a right to inclusive liturgy', https://uscatholic.org/articles/202404/women-have-a-right-to-inclusive-liturgy.

Beckford, Martin, 2023, 'Archbishop of York Rev Stephen Cottrell says that starting the Lord's Prayer with 'Our Father' is problematic', https://www.dailymail.co.uk/news/article-12276651/Archbishop-York-Rev-Stephen-Cottrell-says-Father-problematic.html.

Capetillo-Ventura, Nelly C., Jalil-Pérez, Sarith I., Motilla-Negrete, Karla, 2015, 'Gender dysphoria: An overview', *Medicina Universitaria*, Vol. 17, No. 66, pp. 53–8, https://www.researchgate.net/publication/282524260_Gender_dysphoria_An_overview.

'Church of England Considers Gender Neutral Language for God', 2023, https://www.nytimes.com/2023/02/09/world/europe/england-church-gender-neutral-god.html.

The Church of England, 1969, Section B, "Divine Service and the Administration of the Sacraments", https://www.churchofengland.org/about/leadership-and-governance/legal-services/canons-church-england/section-b#b14.

Clare-Young, Alex, 2024, *Faith in Transition*, https://www.youtube.com/watch?v=XyY55hlvDAM.

Conger, George, 2016, 'Christa returns to Cathedral of St John the Divine, https://anglican.ink/2016/10/06/christa-returns-to-cathedral-of-st-john-the-divine/.

Crozier-De Rosa, Sharon, 2024, 'What are the four waves of feminism? And what comes next?', https://theconversation.com/what-are-the-four-waves-of-feminism-and-what-comes-next-224153.

Crux, Elise Ann Allen, 2024, 'Pope turns to female theologians for advice on women's roles in Church, https://catholicherald.co.uk/pope-turns-to-female-theologians-on-womens-roles-in-church/.

Dodd, Vikram, 2024, 'Violence against women a "national emergency" in England and Wales, police say', https://www.theguardian.com/society/article/2024/jul/23/violence-against-women-national-emergency-england-wales-police.

French, Daniel, 2023, 'God the "Father" isn't sexist', https://www.spectator.co.uk/article/god-the-father-isnt-sexist/.

Gendertrust.org.uk, 2025, 'Gender concepts around the world', https://www.gendertrust.org.uk/gender-concepts-around-the-world/.

Guite, Malcolm, 2015, 'O Sapientia An Advent Antiphon', https://malcolmguite.files.wordpress.com/2016/12/17-o-sapienta.jpg.

Higgins, Charlotte, 2018, "The age of patriarchy: how an unfashionable idea became a rallying cry for feminism today', https://www.theguardian.com/news/2018/jun/22/the-age-of-patriarchy-how-an-unfashionable-idea-became-a-rallying-cry-for-feminism-today.

Khomami, Nadia, 2015, 'Let God be a "she", says Church of England women's group', www.theguardian.com/world/2015/jun/01/church-of-england-womens-group-bishops.

Langley, Jonathan, 23 August 2024, 'Three chords and the truth', *Church Times*, https://www.churchtimes.co.uk/articles/2024/23-august/features/features/three-chords-and-the-truth-folk-musicians-push-the-boundaries.

'Lord's Prayer (Alternate Version from the New Zealand Book of Prayer)', https://livinghour.org/lords-prayer/new-zealand-maori/.

OrdainWomen, 2024, 'Diakonia and Determination: A prayer of lament, hope and witness for inclusive Holy Orders', https://www.youtube.com/watch?v=dfY_FAoOwFw.

The Methodist Church, 2023, 'The Methodist Church Inclusive Language Guide', https://media.methodist.org.uk/media/documents/ILG_designed_update_October_2023v2.pdf.

Monasteries of the Heart, https://www.monasteriesoftheheart.org/.

Mowczko, Marg, 2013, 'The Human ('Ha'adam'), Man (ish) and Woman (Ishshah) in Genesis 2', https://margmowczko.com/human-man-woman-genesis-2/.

National Policing Statement 2024 For Violence Against Women and Girls (VAWG) – July 2024, WEBSITE PUBLICATION-2, https://news.npcc.police.uk/resources/vteb9-ec4cx-7xgru-wufru-5vvo6.

Orchard Ridge, 1993, 'Our Father, Our Mother: Parallel versions', https://worshipwords.co.uk/our-father-our-mother-parallel-versions-orchard-ridge-wisconsin-usa/.

Oremus, Will, 2014, 'Here are all the genders you can be on Facebook', https://slate.com/technology/2014/02/facebook-custom-gender-options-here-are-all-56-custom-options.html.

Oxford English Dictionary, 2013m 'they', https://www.oed.com/dictionary/they_pron?tl=true.

PA Media, 2023, 'Church of England to consider use of gender neutral terms for God', https://www.theguardian.com/world/2023/feb/07/church-of-england-to-consider-use-of-gender-neutral-terms-for-god.

Plan UK, 2024, 'The state of girls' rights in the UK', https://plan-uk.org/state-of-girls-rights.

Ruff, Anthony, 2016, '"Christa" – The Female Christ on the Cross – is Back!', https://www.praytellblog.com/index.php/2016/10/05/christa-the-female-christ-on-the-cross-is-back/.

Shea, Matt, 2023, 'Andrew Tate: the Man who Groomed the World?', broadcast on BBC 3, 31 August 2023; also available in 2024 on https://www.bbc.co.uk/iplayer/episodes/m001q1nf/andrew-tate.

Smithers, Christopher, 2023, 'Archbishop suggests God is gender neutral, which might come as a surprise to God', https://www.express.co.uk/comment/expresscomment/1789426/our-father-lords-prayer-sexist-gender-neutral-Archbishop-of-York-General-Synod.

Spring, Marianna, 2024, "It stains your brain': How social media algorithms show violence to boys', BBC Panorama, https://www.bbc.co.uk/news/articles/c4gdqzxypdzo.

Swerling, Gabriella, 2023, 'Calling God "our Father" is problematic, says Archbishop of York', https://www.telegraph.co.uk/news/2023/07/07/calling-god-father-problematic-archbishop-york-gender/.

Women and the Church, https://www.womenandthechurch.org/.

Women's Ordination Worldwide', https://womensordinationcampaign.org/.

Music

Barrett, Ally, Hymns, https://reverendally.org/reverendallys-hymns/.
Chittister, Joan, Benedictine spirituality, https://www.monasteriesofthe heart.org/prayer-feminist-liturgy-joan-chittister.
The Como Mamas, 2014, 'Out of the wilderness', https://thecomomamas.bandcamp.com/track/out-of-the-wilderness.
Iona community, 2005, 'I Will Sing a Song of Love', on *I Will Not Sing Alone*, Wild Goose Publications, https://www.ionabooks.com/product/i-will-sing-a-song-of-love-downloadable-music-track/.
Iona community, 1995, 'Lord, to Whom Shall We Go', on *Come All You People*, Wild Goose Publications, https://www.ionabooks.com/product/lord-to-whom-shall-we-go-reading-downloadable-music-track/.
Iona community, 2014, 'No Wind at the Window: Carol of the Annunciation', Wild Goose Publications, https://www.youtube.com/watch?v=A40RuvTSjWA; and 1992, https://hymnary.org/text/no_wind_at_the_window.
The King's Singers, 2012, 'Weep O Mine Eyes', *Royal Rhymes and Rounds*, https://www.youtube.com/watch?v=totNCMNNXQ8.
MacMillan, James, 2019, 'O Radiant Dawn', *O Radiant Dawn*, Apollo 5, https://www.youtube.com/watch?v=5drCQq73ZBE.
Rizza, Margaret, 2003 'Veni Sancte Spiritus', in *Light in our Darkness: Simple Chants and Psalms*, Kevin Mayhew, https://www.google.com/search?q=Rizza%2C+Margaret%2C+2003+%E2%80%98Veni+Sancte+Spiritus%E2%80%99.
Schutte, Dan, 2000, 'I, the Lord of Sea and Sky', *Common Praise: A new edition of Hymns Ancient and Modern*, No. 470, Canterbury: Canterbury Press, https://www.google.com/search?q=Schutte%2C+Dan%2C+2000%2C+%E2%80%98I%2C+the+Lord+of+Sea+and+Sky.
Siskin Green, 2023, 'Will your anchor hold?', https://siskingreen.bandcamp.com/album/siskin-green.
Stewart, Louise, Director of Multitude of Voyces, https://www.multitudeofvoyces.co.uk.
Tatlow, Anita and Ben, 2022, Salt of the Sound, 'Grounded', 'Peace, With You' and 'Vespers', on *Meditations*, Vol. 5, Echoes Blue Music, https://saltofthesound.bandcamp.com/album/meditations-vol-5.
Tatlow, Anita and Ben, Salt of the Sound, 2024, *Meditations*, Vol. 6, Echoes Blue Music, https://saltofthesound.bandcamp.com/album/meditations-vol-6.
Tavener, John, 2020, 'Mother of God, here I stand', https://www.youtube.com/watch?v=UnS1mRAd57I&feature=youtu.be.
Women and the Church, Prayers, https://www.womenandthechurch.org/ and https://static1.squarespace.com/static/66bf1dc1965d122bd4d4e247/t/66f54968cfeeac57411ddba5/1727351144922/Prayers.pdf.
Wood, Sheryl and Edwards Grant, 2020, 'O Wisdom, Breathed from God', from anonymous sixth–seventh-century text, https://www.youtube.com/watch?v=moMPbx5MUdw.

Appendix

Church of England Canon Law

Introduction

At ordination and licensing, all Anglican clergy swear an oath to 'use only the forms of service which are authorized or allowed by Canon' (Declaration of Assent, *Common Worship: Services and Prayers*, p. xi in *New Patterns for Worship (NPW)*, p. 51; and Earey, 2011, p. 14). What is less well known is how much creative freedom is permitted, a freedom I will outline here. I will begin with a reminder about the legal structures.

Canon Law

Under Canon B1, it is a requirement to use the services provided by the Church. In the first instance, this means those contained in the Book of Common Prayer (BCP). Canons B2 and B4, however, permit further services to be authorised, usually by Synod or ('for use on certain occasions') by the Convocations, Archbishops or 'Ordinary' (the person with ordinary authority over a Diocese or similar area – usually the Bishop) and these are contained within *Common Worship: Services and Prayers* (CW) (Section B, 'Divine Service and the Administration of the Sacraments' and NPW, pp. 51–2). It is also possible to produce services which are neither in the BCP, nor authorized under Canons B2 and B4. This is covered by Canon B5, which authorizes ministers to use their 'discretion' to 'make and use variations ... in any form of service authorized by Canon B1'. There is thus discretionary freedom to create new material, but, as might be expected, this is within limits.

What are these limits? Changes must be 'not of substantial importance' (not defined, as noted by Earey, 2011, p. 18). Furthermore, 'All variations in forms of service and all forms of service used under this Canon shall be reverent and seemly and shall be neither contrary to, nor indicative of any departure from, the doctrine of the Church of England in any essential matter' (Section B; see also Tarrant, 2012, pp. 9–10).

Doctrine has, of course, a long history of disputation and interpretation. So, what are the authoritative sources of Church of England doctrine?

Canon A5, drawing on the Worship and Doctrine Measure 1974, section 5(1), which authorizes alternative forms of services to those in the BCP, gives us our answer. It states that the doctrine of the Church of England is, 'Grounded in the Holy Scriptures, and in such teachings of the ancient Fathers and Councils of the Church as are agreeable to the said Scriptures.' (Note the room for doubt and the prevalence given to Scripture in such a case.) 'In particular such doctrine is to be found in the Thirty-Nine Articles of Religion, The Book of Common Prayer, and the Ordinal'. These are given special, authoritative prominence (NPW, p. 52).

To assist in determining whether an element of liturgy is contrary to the doctrine of the Church of England in any essential matter, reference should thus be made to these sources.

Eucharistic Prayers (excluding prefaces), Confession and Absolution (although see the caveat below) and Creeds and Affirmations of Faith have all touched on areas of doctrinal controversy and therefore authorized material must be used (Earey, 2011, pp. 16–17).

Freedoms within Canon Law

Mark Earey and Phillip Tovey remind us, however, that Common Worship was intended to facilitate considerable flexibility and creativity and that the Service of the Word, in particular, was 'revolutionary'. *New Patterns for Worship* was published in 2002 to assist with accessing these freedoms. It provides a 'prophetic' resource 'designed to set people free and to enable change', but instead there has been a tendency to become trapped in existing patterns (2009, pp. 7, 12, 17, 20).

While we need to use *Authorized* material for services from the BCP or else approved by General Synod, for other services we may use *Allowed* material (Earey, 2011, pp. 15–16). The House of Bishops offer 'commended' material in these cases, either whole services or parts of services. This can include seasonal intercessions, blessings and introductions to the peace. There is also an 'unofficial' category which remains 'allowed'. This includes songs, hymns, prayers and other liturgical material that does not require authorization, but which has not been particularly commended. In this areas, a local decision can be made by the minister and/or the Parochial Church Council. Iona and other liturgical material of this nature would fit in this category and this is the place where our own writing is acceptable.

To clarify, we may compose our own material in the following:

- Introduction to confession.
- Kyrie confessions.
- Collect.
- Gospel acclamations.
- Intercessions.
- Introduction to the peace.
- Prefaces to Eucharistic prayers.
- Blessings and endings.
- Service of the Word (with or without Holy Communion).

Introduction to confession

In the rubric for the introduction to confession in Holy Communion Order One, we are told, 'A minister uses a seasonal invitation to confession or these or other suitable words' (CW, 2000, p. 168). 'Suitable' is not defined, so will simply require us to follow the general guidelines of being reverent, seemly and observing Church of England doctrine. Earey also suggests that we can assess 'suitable' by 'comparison with the sort of thing which CW itself gives us' (2013, p. 73).

Kyrie confessions

While confession and absolution is a sensitive area, meaning that Anglicans must, in the main, use authorized versions of confession and absolution, an exception is the provision to write 'short penitential sentences between the petitions of the *Kyrie*' (NPW, p. 75), so long as an authorized absolution follows (NPW, pp. 76–7; CW 2000, p. 133). Examples are given in *CW Services and Prayers* (pp. 133–4) and NPW (pp. 91–4). It is not expected that these be the norm on Sundays, however (Earey, 2011, p. 331).

Collects

The Collects are an authorized set of texts, providing an alternative to those in the BCP. As Earey notes (2011, p. 44), the rubric to Holy Communion Order One simply says 'The Collect is said' (CW, 2000, p. 171), assuming an authorized text, and indeed is marked with an asterisk in *A Service of the Word with a Celebration of Holy Communion*, indicating it 'must follow an authorized text' (CW, 2000, p. 25). However, the introduction suggests that the Collect 'does not have to be that of the day; it may be a thematic one based on the readings ... or be used to sum up the Prayers'. This, Earey suggests, 'presumably allows for a locally composed text or one from a non-authorized source' (2011, p. 44; Tarrant, 2012, p. 12).

He concludes that, although we are given a 'strong steer towards using one of the authorized texts', Canon B5 can liberate us to make changes which are not of substantial importance (2011, p. 44). NPW provides good guidance for writing a Collect for a particular theme, situation or service, which supports this conclusion. One of their suggestions includes the admonition to, 'Use language which includes women as well as men, black as well as white' (p. 176).

Gospel acclamations

We are free to add an acclamation to herald the Gospel reading. Examples for Ordinary Time are given in *CW Services and Prayers* (Ordinary Time, p. 280, and Seasonal Provisions, p. 300) but, Earey notes (2011, p. 56), 'others can be devised drawing from appropriate passages of Scripture'.

Intercessions

Intercessory prayer offers an opportunity for full creativity, and is one of the few areas where this freedom has been fully taken advantage of. While there are guidelines for what makes good intercessions (including CW, 2000, pp. 281–7; Plater, 1995; Sayer, 1997, 1999 and 2000), the content is very open.

Introduction to the Peace

The rubric in CW *Services and Prayers* for Holy Communion Order One (p. 175) states: 'The president may introduce the Peace with a suitable sentence.'

Eucharistic prayers

We have a wide range of Eucharistic prayers to choose from, including eight in Order One (See Earey, 2011, p. 58 for the full list) with two additional prayers for use when there are a large number of children present.[1] In addition, prefaces, Earey reminds us, may be adapted to ensure the Eucharistic prayer is 'seasonal or appropriate to the theme of the service'.

Short Proper Prefaces 'are added to the end of the praise section of the prayer, between the opening dialogue and the Sanctus' and, in the Anglican context, may be inserted in Eucharistic Prayers A, B and C in Order One. *Extended Prefaces* 'replace the whole of the praise section of the prayer between the opening dialogue and the Sanctus.' These are used within Eucharistic Prayers A, B and E for Order One. Optional acclamations can be added for Prayers A and F (Earey, 2011, p. 58; CW, 2000, p. 333). You can find options for both of these in *Common Worship: Services and Prayers* (2000) covering both ordinary (p. 294) and seasonal time (pp. 300–29). It is also worth checking out CW *Times and Seasons* and *Festivals*. Mark Earey is helpful in the detail of how to apply these to particular Eucharistic Prayers (2011, pp. 58–9). *New Patterns for Worship* (NPW) also contains short prefaces

---

1 At https://www.churchofengland.org/prayer-and-worship/worship-texts-and-resources/common-worship/holy-communion/additional-eucharistic (accessed 3 August 25).

and a wide range of Thanksgivings, which can be adapted to make extended prefaces and gives advice about how to use these and also on how to produce your own prefaces (pp. 258–67, 234–57, 222).

A good way to prepare to write one's own preface is to read the available prefaces in *Common Worship: Services and Prayers* (Order One, pp. 184–205; Order One Traditional Language, pp. 216–19; and seasonal provisions, pp. 294 and 300–29), and then consider which aspect of God's saving power you wish to emphasize in your own preface. See also Section G on Praise and Thanksgiving in NPW (pp. 242, 251, 258–67). Other denominations will, of course, have their own resources.

Blessings and endings

The rubric for the Dismissal in Holy Communion Order One (CW, 2000, p. 183) suggests: 'The president may use the seasonal blessing, or another suitable blessing.'

Service of the Word (SOTW)

The service that offers the most room for creativity is the SOTW, with or without Holy Communion. This can be used for non-Eucharistic services on Sundays, as a framework for Daily Prayer and also as the framework for Holy Communion (although not normally the regular Sunday service). The exact requirements varying accordingly and can be found in Earey, 2011, pp. 49–50. The requirements for a weekday SOTW are minimal: the Lord's Prayer must be included and Scripture readings and prayers for the Church and the world are expected, but the content of these is open; in addition, there is no prescribed shape or structure (Earey, 2013, p. 73; and 2011, pp. 47–50, 53. See also NPW, pp. 9–20; CW, 2000, pp. 21–7).

The following is a useful framework (from NPW, p. 11), although it can be varied.

Preparation

Greeting
Prayers of Pentitence
Venite, Kyries, Glorias, hymn, song, or set of responses may be used
Collect here or in the prayers

The Liturgy of the Word

Reading/s
Psalm
Sermon
Creed or affirmation of faith

Prayers

Intercessions and thanksgivings
The Lord's Prayer

Conclusion

Blessing / dismissal / other liturgical ending

Baptisms, Weddings and Funerals

Although not the focus of this guide, it is worth noting that there are considerable freedoms in the occasional offices. These are identified by careful reading of the rubrics, identifying instructions like 'such as' and 'may', which permit creative licence.

Additional freedoms

There are some additional flexibilities 'hidden in plain sight' within *Common Worship*.

- The alternative doxology (CW, 2005, p. 648), 'Glory to God, Source of all being, Eternal Word and Holy Spirit', can be substituted for the traditional doxology in the Psalter.
- During Ordinary Time, one may choose texts from outside the lectionary (Earey 2011, p. 34; NPW, Section C, pp. 103–4), including those in which women are prominent.
- Ecumenical Canons B43 and B44 permit some of the normal requirements of worship to be dispensed with in an ecumenical setting (Earey, 2013, p. 57; 2011, p. 18).
- The Bishop may permit other flexibility for missional reasons, for example in Fresh Expressions.

Conclusion

There is considerably more freedom for Anglicans writing their own material than is often realised, and we can find these by attending to the rubrics and notes for each service.

www.ingramcontent.com/pod-product-compliance
Lightning Source LLC
Chambersburg PA
CBHW060615080526
44585CB00013B/833